Once Upon Another Time

They were a very diverse lot. Some were believers, others atheists. Some were rightwingers, others belonged to the left. They were coming to give lectures, bring books and smuggle writings and messages from us back to their lands. We did not necessarily agree with all of them. But the thrill of having an opponent who really believes what he is saying and who believes the same about you was an ambrosia for us who lived in a totalitarian environment where anything else than parroting the Big Brother's lie was dangerous...

PAVEL BRATINKA, Prague, 1999

Communism is the secret name of the dread antagonist setting proletarian rule with all its consequences against the present bourgeois regime. It will be a frightful duel. How will it end? No one knows but gods and goddesses acquainted with the future. We know only this much: Communism, though little discussed now and loitering in hidden garrets on miserable straw pallets, is the dark hero destined for a great, if temporary role in the modern world...

HEINRICH HEINE, Paris, 20 June 1842

To Dermod
with best wishes.
Jessica Douglas Home

JESSICA
DOUGLAS-HOME

Once Upon Another Time

VENTURES BEHIND THE
IRON CURTAIN

*

MICHAEL RUSSELL

© Jessica Douglas-Home 2000

First published in Great Britain 2000
by Michael Russell (Publishing) Ltd
Wilby Hall, Wilby, Norwich NR16 2JP

Typeset in Sabon by Waveney Typesetters,
Wymondham, Norfolk
Printed and bound in Great Britain
by Biddles Ltd, Guildford and King's Lynn

ISBN 0 85955 259 4

With acknowledgements to Faber and Faber Ltd
for the quotation on pp. 22–3 from
Open Letters: Selected Prose of Václav Havel

Acknowledgements

I am very grateful to Agnieszka Kolakowska and Barbara Day for reading through the chapters on Poland and Czechoslovakia respectively, to Christian Mititelu and Hugh Arbuthnott for reading those on Romania, and to Richard Cohen and Alex Maccormick for their early editing suggestions.

Roger Scruton made innumerable helpful suggestions, nearly all of which are reflected one way or another in the final text. My final heartfelt thanks go to Rodney Leach who, whenever I felt like giving up, encouraged me to continue and devoted meticulous care to helping me revise and make improvements. It was of particular importance to me that he enjoyed discussing and analysing all the people who feature prominently in the text.

Prologue

In 1997, seven years after Ceauşescu's downfall and execution, I received a telephone call from Claudiu Secaşiu, a historian I knew from the dissident days in Romania. He spoke in the same hushed, conspiratorial voice that I remembered. 'Extracts from the secret police files have just been published. You figure prominently in them. They call you a very dangerous lady – *o doamnă foarte periculoasă*. I think you should come here and try to see the originals.'

My mind leaped back in time. The chance of gaining access to these files must surely be slim. Romania had taken longer than any other country in the Soviet bloc to rid itself of its old guard. Ceauşescu's former henchman Ion Iliescu had only recently been voted out of office. Now Emil Constantinescu was in power, but had mysteriously failed to dismiss the head of the Securitate, the secret police. Although Iliescu had supposedly 'humanised' the Securitate, in practice fifty percent of its officers remained in place, the other fifty percent having been replaced by nobodies paid to put on a genial appearance. There was, however, one significant new development. A member of Constantinescu's party had been put in charge of the warehouse where the Securitate documents were stored. He was a friend of Secaşiu. It was worth a try.

Within three weeks – after being led down several blind alleys – I was in Bucharest's military zone with the files in my hands. As I turned over these extraordinary documents, dates, conversations, atmosphere flooded back to me. I lived again the horror of Ceauşescu's Romania. During those clandestine meetings ten years before, in Bucharest, Iaşi, Cluj and Braşov, none of our tiny group had had the slightest inkling of an end to the oppression. We were threatened. We were tracked and bugged. And what happened to us, the messengers from a free country, was nothing to the daily suffering of our Romanian contacts. To read the transcripts was to re-enact in safety the most intense and precarious part of my life.

But my story does not start in Romania.

It was my husband Charles Douglas-Home's arrest and inter-rogation in Czechoslovakia that first brought home to me the meaning of the Iron Curtain. Charlie had started his journalis-tic career on the *Daily Express* in the '60s and was now the defence correspondent of *The Times*. In those early days of our marriage his job took him all over the world, often at a few hours' notice. The previous year he had covered the Six Day War in Israel. In July 1968 he was sent to Czechoslovakia, where 25,000 Russian troops were on manoeuvre in the Slovak countryside.

Telephone conversations being impossible, Charlie's vivid articles were my sole source of information about him. The headlines signalled growing alarm – 'Soviet Troops' Role in War of Nerves' from Košice; 'Czech Crisis: Russians Linger in Slovakia' from Žilina. What made the stories ominous was that there had recently been stirrings of independence and civil lib-erty in Czechoslovakia under its new President Dubček. They called it the 'Prague Spring'. To Western eyes Dubček's doctrine of 'socialism with a human face' hardly seemed a threat to Moscow. But still the Soviet troops, hidden in the woods of eastern Slovakia, refused to leave.

I was just starting a six-week summer season job in Folke-stone as a theatre designer. The year before, I had been given an Arts Council scholarship to work as an assistant designer in Bromley and York, but this time I would be responsible for planning and executing my own sets. These were the twilight days of repertory. Each week designers built and painted new sets, actors and actresses mastered new scripts, and audiences throughout the provinces were treated to an extraordinary range of comedies, melodramas and musicals. My ambition was to be a painter and initially I had taken up stage design only to earn a living. But the theatre entered my blood.

Pregnant and feeling sick each morning, I left my bed-and-breakfast and treated myself, though I could barely afford it, to a hotel in the centre of the town. In the evenings, exhausted after laying out layer upon layer of background paint on 18 ft flats, I would watch television in the open plan lounge-cum-hallway. One night news came of Charlie's arrest as a 'spy' by a Soviet armoured unit in the Tatra mountains above Bratislava. For the two days of his captivity I was kept informed of events by the foreign editor of *The Times*. Charlie's predicament made headline news and I told myself that the Soviets would not want to cause a diplomatic crisis by maltreating a British subject. I naively believed, too, that *The Times* was probably influential enough to ensure his safety.

On the other hand there might be scope for a show trial, in which a newspaper correspondent with a well-known name was exposed and convicted. My rush of relief when Charlie was released showed me how worried I had been. I took the weekend off and went to London to be with him. When I returned to the hotel on the Monday I was politely told that there was no room for me. Seeing an almost empty page in the register, I asked for an explanation. With embarrassment, the clerk told me that the management could not accept as a guest the wife of a man who had been arrested. For the first time it dawned on me how many decent people had no conception of the realities of life behind the Iron Curtain.

Meanwhile, Charlie was working to a tight deadline on a description of his experience. He had been dragged from his car by Russian soldiers toting machine guns, an operation made more alarming because in their eagerness to lay hands on him they had omitted to undo his seat belt and mistook his immobility for resistance. After a rough eight-hour interrogation, he had been taken to the Austrian border and dumped on the roadside.

[11]

Pleased by Charlie's piece, the editor gave him four days' holiday, which he spent hay-making in Gloucestershire. Alone in Folkestone, I started to read every book I could find about Eastern Europe. Within weeks the Russian Army entered Prague, closed down any institutions which had responded favourably to the more liberal political mood, arrested President Dubček and reimposed Soviet control. Few of us who - followed those events would forget the desolation that we felt for the Czechs. The tanks driving through the capital, the mournful crowds resigned to their return to captivity, the hopeless heroism of the few who resisted, the tragedy of Jan Palach, the student who set himself alight in impotent protest – these were images which would not go away.

For the moment, however, painting, theatre design and bringing up my children were my priorities. We had two sons, Tara in 1969 and Luke in 1971. I had my first solo exhibitions, and Charlie worked his way up to foreign editor, then deputy editor. After Rupert Murdoch bought *The Times* in 1981 there was a chaotic twelve months, at the end of which he dismissed his new editor and put Charlie in his place. For a long while I had not much involved myself in political issues, but the Soviet occupation of Afghanistan, then much in the news, reawakened all the emotions that had wracked me after Charlie's experience in 1968. I found myself turning again to the leader pages of the newspapers.

One

In the autumn of 1982, Charlie brought home from the office the first issue of a new magazine. I was attracted by its dull, understated cover and old-fashioned typography. It carried essays by, or about, thinkers of whom I knew little – Michael Oakeshott, Karl Popper, Friedrich Hayek, Leszek Kolakowski. At a time when it was generally assumed that intellectualism was the special property of the left, I was electrified by this school of political philosophers, with their compelling demolition of socialism and their shocking belief in free markets.

The article which interested me most in that first copy of the *Salisbury Review* was an anonymous editorial on Eastern Europe. By 1982 the Kremlin had integrated the satellite countries into a monolithic economic bloc, taken over their organs of state and installed hundreds of thousands of occupying troops. Intermittent rebellions – Hungary in 1956, Prague in 1968 and Solidarity's recent uprising in Poland – had been ruthlessly put down. Hundreds had fled and written books in exile. But what of those who stayed behind?

Buried beneath the monolith of Communism, the European spirit survives, in clandestine organisations, in the Church, in secret societies and unofficial publications, through which the memory of a European identity is kept alive. With the universal, but impotent, rejection of Communism, the people of Eastern Europe have begun increasingly to envisage themselves as primarily Europeans, whose history has been arbitrarily severed from the root to which it was once attached. The attempt to keep open the channels through which a small but sufficient nourishment can reach the severed limb is one which must arouse our admiration and support.

I learned from the article that although the nature of the oppression was similar throughout the Soviet bloc, the nature of the resistance was diverse.

National identities had not, after all, been obliterated. Each country found its own way, rooted in its own history, to keep hope alive.

I was introduced to Roger Scruton, the editor of the *Review*, by the cool and exotic Diana Phipps, a Czech émigrée who lived in Connaught Square in west London. Her seductiveness was accentuated by her voice, with its low, soft, elongated vowels, which Charlie and I competed with each other to imitate. Her family, which had survived wars and changing rulers in Bohemia for nearly a thousand years, had been finally forced out of Czechoslovakia in 1948 – long after the rest of the landed aristocracy had fled – when Diana was eleven. After a peripatetic childhood and a brief and tragic marriage in America she had moved to London in the 1960s. There she entertained and encouraged artists and intellectuals in a most un-British salon.

Roger Scruton's wild, coldly detached appearance, his unorthodox opinions and his brilliant academic gifts appealed to Diana. He had a strongly proportioned, pale face, with blue eyes barred by gold-rimmed spectacles, and a huge thicket of wiry red hair that shot out in all directions. From his father Jack, a class warrior rescued from the slums of Manchester by service in the RAF, he had inherited a disposition to strong opinions, though the principles that each held so dearly served only to turn father and son into dedicated adversaries.

As a university lecturer, Roger was practised at holding an audience. The evening I met him he sat in silence at Diana's dinner table for an hour, somewhat intimidated by her, before being drawn into talking about the situation in Eastern Europe. The result was a three-minute *tour de force*, in the course of which I gathered that he was one of a small group of philosophers who travelled to Prague to meet Czech dissidents in secret. He evidently knew many of them personally. Longing to know more of this Pimpernel world, I made an appointment to meet him next day at Birkbeck College, where he described what amounted to nothing short of a catacomb university existing under the nose of the Communist authorities. He gave me a reading list and an article written by a dissident which he thought might interest Charlie for *The Times*. It appeared on the centre page in June 1983 under the heading 'No Peace Without Freedom' by 'a citizen of Prague'.

The anonymous writer was Petr Pithart, who worked as a daytime office-cleaner in Prague and was later to become Prime Minister of the Czech and Slovak Federation. Pithart urged his Western readers not to be taken in by the International Peace Movement, which was no more than a Communist Party front, but instead to speak up for the dissidents. In Czechoslovakia the true representatives of peace were the Charter 77 signatories, many of whom were serving long prison sentences for seeking to hold the state to the human rights commitments it had entered into in the Helsinki Accords of 1975.

The contact between Roger's group and the dissidents traced its origins to a maverick Czech philosopher, Julius Tomin, whose letter to the Philosophy Faculty in Oxford inviting speakers for his seminars had arrived in 1979. Braving police violence and trumped up charges of clinical paranoia, Tomin had instituted a series of open but unofficial academic courses, principally attended by students excluded from Prague's Charles University on political grounds. He had written to other universities, too, but Oxford was the only one to respond.

First to go out was a tutor at St Hilda's, Kathy Wilkes, followed soon after by a Canadian philosopher and political activist of redoubtable intellect and energy, Chuck Taylor. The hub of the Oxford effort was Balliol College, and Anthony

Kenny, the Master of Balliol, himself went out in 1980. While Kenny was analysing a passage in which Aristotle argued that the philosophical life was unique in being almost impossible to take away, twenty policemen barged their way in to Tomin's apartment and arrested him.

The newspapers took up the story of Kenny's interrogation and expulsion. The public's imagination was caught and letters of sympathy stuffed with five and ten pound notes poured into Balliol. For a while nobody could think what to do with the money. Eventually Kathy Wilkes and Roger Scruton, who had joined the group from London University, came up with the idea of establishing a charitable trust to support a proper programme of visits. They called it the Jan Hus Foundation, after the thirteenth-century Czech reformer and martyr.

The brutal encounters of Tomin and his pupils with the secret police led to soul-searching about the form that the British visits should take. Tomin himself dropped out of the reckoning, leaving Czechoslovakia permanently for Oxford, but Stephen Lukes, another Balliol don, had made several friendships among dissident Czechs, which were to prove invaluable. In the end Lukes decided not to become a trustee, leaving five of the rest of the academics to design the programme. Together they shared the task of taking money, books and journals to Prague and arranging the seminars. I asked Roger Scruton if I could come to their next meeting in September.

A few weeks later four philosophers laden with bottles of wine trooped into the study of Roger's dark Bayswater flat. The room was crammed from floor to ceiling with books. There was some sparse mahogany furniture, a piano stacked with music stood in one corner. I was captivated by the diversity of the trustees – the suavely cosmopolitan Alan Montefiore, the forthright Kathy Wilkes, Bill Newton-Smith with his urbane, Canadian sense of humour, and Ralph Walker exuding a strict Scottish morality and a no-nonsense attitude. The Foundation's business began round Roger's dining room table. His view was that work should be combined with good food and good claret, but the agenda was strictly practical. There were assets of £5,000 and bankers' orders from several wellwishers, including Tom Stoppard and Iris Murdoch. I noticed that Diana, who had vowed she would never return to Czechoslovakia and on the surface distanced herself from the tragedy that had befallen her country, had been giving periodic sums of £500.

As I listened to the minutes of the previous meeting, a shadowy picture began to emerge of individuals with unfamiliar names. Frequent references to *samizdat* – a word I had previously associated only with Soviet clandestine publication – permeated the discussion. Recent visitors' reports elicited ideas of new contacts to develop, new texts to edit, translate or publish, new lists of books and articles to transmit. The most important decisions concerned the planning of the schedule of lectures in Prague for the next academic year. I listened to each item in silence, waiting for my moment. It was clear that their Czech contacts were interested in far more than philosophy. I said I was willing to help on theatre and the arts. I would learn the ropes by taking out books and money with the next visitor. By the end of the evening I had achieved my ambition: a date for my first mission behind the Iron Curtain. It was to be October 1983. I had just three weeks in which to prepare myself.

Two

I arrived at Prague airport at noon. Distinctly nervous about the philosophy books in my hand luggage and the £600 cash in my wallet, I made for the Nothing to Declare exit. My heart was racing. I saw ahead a sullen peak-capped official slouching behind a grey plastic table. 'What is your reason to be here?' he asked. 'I'm an artist,' I replied, 'I've come to see the Impressionist collection in your National Gallery.' He marked my bag with chalk and sourly gestured me through. I disguised my relief with a studied air of indifference, suddenly almost over-confident. How needless to have been scared, I told myself, by Charlie's half-teasing reminder about Gerald Brooke, the Englishman who had been arrested in Moscow and imprisoned for five years in a labour camp for importing bibles.

In what seemed no time at all, my bus reached the city centre. Roger Scruton was coming by train from Vienna and I was to meet him in the café Obecní Dům near Charles University. As it turned out it was he who was searched at the border. Two guards entered his compartment, ordered him to open his suitcases and confiscated all his books.

Our mission was to call on four of Prague's leading dissidents, the moving spirits of Czechoslovakia's 'underground university'. Other outlawed scholars would be in the shadows waiting to make contact with us if it was safe to do so. This secret academic network had copied Communist tactics with a system of cells within cells. None of the participants had more information about the others than was absolutely necessary. It was too dangerous even for the leaders to be in possession of every name. We ourselves never knew how many were involved.

Early that afternoon Roger and I set out for the north of the city. Our first rendezvous was with Dr Ladislav Hejdánek. Leaving our luggage in the Zlatá Husa hotel in Wenceslas Square (the 'square' is in fact a wide boulevard sloping up to the statue of King Wenceslas), we walked a mile and a half on cobbled pavements in the hot autumn sun, checking from time to time whether we were being followed. This seemed easy. The streets were almost empty, devoid of chatter and laughter; the few people that we saw had a sluggish, defeated look. After half an hour we passed into what had once been a prosperous district of grey- and beige-stuccoed late-nineteenth-century houses. As we drew nearer to where Hejdánek lived, I felt a surge of anticipation. He stood very high in the estimation of Roger, Kathy Wilkes and Alan Montefiore.

A minute or so after our knock on the door, a dignified, thick-set Slavonic figure appeared, gently beckoning us into a good-sized sitting room, into which the light poured from tall windows. The furniture seemed to have been inherited from the 1920s; it had that dated air of objects which until the quite recent past had been consciously modern. Hejdánek moved slowly and stiffly. I thought at first that his bent figure was due to age, but when I looked closer at his smooth complexion and light brown hair I realised that he must be suffering from some infirmity.

His grave demeanour did not disguise his pleasure at seeing us, evident in his eyes and his attentive nods as our conversation proceeded slowly in halting English interspersed with German. With a sign of his hand he indicated that we should keep our voices low. He did not know the location of the electronic bugging equipment in his flat, or who had installed it – probably a state 'repair man' entering the premises on a false pretext. But the detailed information the police possessed each time he was hauled in for questioning could only have been obtained from listening in to him at home.

For two years Hejdánek had held a weekly Monday evening philosophy seminar. His pupils were students barred from university, dismissed teachers, priests who had been refused a parish. His meetings were well known to the authorities, who were in the habit of raiding them from time to time in a more or less arbitrary manner designed to sow anxiety among the participants. Any Czech caught attending was liable to be gaoled for a few days and subjected to harassment, often in the form of deprivation of housing or education. Most of them, however, had little more to lose and the students continued to arrive in carefully scheduled relays, tiptoeing up the stairs and whispering at the door to gain admission.

We were far from being Hejdánek's only foreign contacts. French, Dutch, Belgians, Americans and Germans had all passed through his door during the year. Jacques Derrida, the *bouffant* French 'deconstructionist', had recently been arrested during a seminar and imprisoned on fabricated charges, until President Mitterrand had secured his release. This incident caused some nervousness among the dissidents' acquaintances in the free world, but it was unusual. The worst that generally befell the visitor from abroad was to be escorted to the airport and put on the first flight out.

In preparation for my visit I had given myself a crash history course, starting from 1918 when the philosopher-statesman Tomáš Masaryk created Czechoslovakia out of the ruins of the Austro-Hungarian Empire after the First World War. Hejdánek had grown up with his country's tragedy. He had been eleven years old in 1938, the year of Munich, when Britain and France condoned the Nazis' annexation of Czechoslovakia's German-speaking region. The next year he had seen the Czech Army surrender to Hitler's panzer divisions without a shot being fired. He was twenty-one in 1948, when the body of Tomáš Masaryk's son Jan, who carried with him the nation's fading hopes of independence, was found in a courtyard thirty feet below his open bathroom window, the victim of police assassins hired by Moscow. As I talked to him about the past, the image came to me of an ancient tree, to which each year had added a new ring of experience.

Arrested in 1952 at the height of Stalinism, Hejdánek lost his academic post as a Protestant theologian; but in the early 1960s, as the political climate improved, he was allowed to publish articles again. For a few brief years young writers began to speak out against censorship; some even dared to advance the arguments for democracy. Hejdánek was able to give up his job as a manual labourer and become that rarest of beings – a Christian philosopher accepted into the Marxist Faculty of Sciences. But in 1968 hope again turned to despair when Brezhnev's tanks entered Prague. For eighteen months he survived, before being dismissed and imprisoned.

On his release, Hejdánek found work as a nightwatchman in the Museum of Literature. But the high cultural standing of the institute forbade any enemy of Communism from being employed in it. He was expelled and became a boiler stoker. In the upside-down world of the Czech intelligentsia this was the most prized job of all, for it guaranteed warmth and uninterrupted time in which to think. Here at last Hejdánek became an active dissident.

It would have been an impertinence to ask him about his personal sufferings, and he volunteered little information about himself. What he wanted to talk about was the work of the underground university. Nobody from Britain had been to his seminars for some time. His respect for British education had been reinforced by the quality of previous lectures. He hoped that would-be visitors had not been frightened off by the Derrida incident and that they would come over more frequently, even if on an irregular basis. His philosophy class of fifteen was incapable of essay-writing. The German style of teaching in Czechoslovakia before the war had not been based on the essay form: as for the Communists, they had reduced their students to note-taking. He wanted a visitor from Britain to set up a proper teaching seminar, with pre-set reading and a lengthy round-table discussion, leading to critical essays, which the class would have to be instructed how to write. For subject matter, he suggested Leibniz, Spinoza, Plato or Aristotle, who provided the basis of his current course-work.

Hejdánek was obviously in pain. He admitted that he had not been able to do as much as he had wanted, but he could not envisage anybody substituting for him and asked whether we could get him some Brufen, an anti-inflammatory painkiller that had helped him in the past. As we walked to our next destination (we went everywhere on foot, so that by the end of this first visit I already knew Prague quite well), Roger told me that Hejdánek had kept his job stoking boilers until 1981, when his spine began to cause him trouble. He could not sit and was eventually too disabled to work. The authorities took the view that a signatory of Charter 77 was not entitled to an invalid's pension. Unless he returned to full-time employment he would face charges of parasitism. The Jan Hus Trustees had tried to raise pension money for him from the Anglican Church and the World Council of Churches, but without success – their declared policy was to work with the regimes in Eastern Europe, not with their victims. He accepted a small sum from us, but made it clear that he would distribute what he received among people even worse placed than himself.

Hejdánek's physical suffering contributed strongly to the impression he gave of dignity and courage. It was my first glimpse of certain qualities I was to encounter again and again in dissidents throughout Eastern Europe – an indefinable spiritual presence and strength which made their privations seem like burdens willingly undertaken for the sake of others. Two years later I came across Paul Wilson's translation of Václav Havel's *The Power of the Powerless* and found words that encapsulated perfectly what I observed each time I went behind the Iron Curtain. Havel describes a Communist society after 'normalisation', when it is no longer necessary to resort to murder or terror to control the population, since everyone has become a collaborator in a self-policing greyness:

The post-totalitarian system touches people at every step, but it does so with its ideological gloves on. That is why life in the system is so thoroughly permeated with hypocrisy and lies: government by bureaucracy is called popular government; the working class is enslaved in the name of the working class; the complete degradation of the individual is presented as his or her ultimate liberation; depriving people of information is called making it available; the use of power to manipulate is called the public control of power, and the arbitrary abuse of power is called observing the legal code; the repression of culture is called its development; the expansion of imperial influence is presented as support for the oppressed; the lack of free expression becomes the highest form of freedom; farcical elections become the highest form of democracy; banning independent thought becomes the most scientific of world views; military occupation becomes fraternal assistance. Because the regime is captive to its own lies, it must falsify everything. It falsifies the past, it falsifies the present and it falsifies the future. It falsifies statistics. It pretends not to possess an omnipotent and unprincipled police apparatus. It pretends to respect human rights. It pretends to persecute no one. It pretends to fear nothing. It pretends to pretend nothing.

Individuals need not believe all these mystifications, but they must behave as though they did, or they must at least tolerate them in silence, or get along with those who work with them. For this reason they must, however, *live within a lie*. They need not accept the lie. It is enough for them to have accepted their life with it and in it. For by this very fact, individuals confirm the system, fulfil the system, make the system, *are* the system.

The decision by Hejdánek and others to take a different path and live a 'life in truth', as Havel – and the philosopher Jan Patočka before him – put it, was what gave us the inspiration to help them.

Three

L ater in the afternoon we walked south across the River Vltava in the autumnal glow of hazy, golden sunlight.

Our next rendezvous, with Petr Pithart, was to be in the apartment of the philosopher and *samizdat* editor Rudolph Kučera, in the Malá Strana district a few yards over the Charles Bridge, just below the castle. Here Roger was due to give a talk on the eighteenth-century politician and philosopher Edmund Burke.

Nothing had prepared me for the beauty of this part of the city. The small houses of artists and the mansions of rich merchants, whose family crests were carved on the top of the doorways or embossed in stucco, stood in confident familiarity among churches and monasteries and the baroque palaces of aristocratic Austro-Hungarian families. The streets and buildings had hardly been touched since the war. On a steep hill, the mellow, ochre-coloured houses still survived where Mozart and Casanova had once lived. There were no neon lights to pollute the view. We threaded our way through street alleys held together by ancient wooden scaffolding which locked at right angles with the stone and appeared to have propped up the buildings for decades.

The richness of Prague's past was matched by the lifelessness of its present – the yellowing plastic tables and concrete floors of dark basement cafés, the drabness of the shops and the slovenliness of the meagre goods on racks and tin shelves; above all, the exhaustion in the demeanour of the people. In a Western city I would have found such sights depressing. Yet here, for reasons which it took me a long time to understand, I was strangely at peace. There were no billboards pushing consumer products at me. Perhaps this was how the wartime London had been that my parents had described to me.

Entering Kučera's seventeenth-century building, we climbed two flights of stone stairs in the back courtyard and knocked on his door. Elongated puppets lined up to greet us in the entrance hall, with big heads, wide, round Czech faces and brightly clothed bodies attached by strings to movable wooden crosses. Rudolf Kučera, the editor of one of Prague's main underground cultural journals, was plump, severe and morose, with deep black unwelcoming eyes. As he talked his hand plucked his face, squeezing his lips and cheeks. His wife Milada, the puppet-maker, smiled sympathetically in the background with their two children.

Petr Pithart had arrived before us. Having been an intermediary over his article for *The Times*, I felt I almost knew him and proudly handed him the £125 he was owed, a small fortune in a country where anything you wanted to buy was available only in foreign exchange shops. I had developed a clear, but as it turned out inaccurate, picture of him. He was more intense and more serious than I had imagined. As a law student, he had been a committed Communist; then in the Prague Spring he became a reformist. But he was shattered by Dubček's downfall and the Soviet reoccupation, and when the time came to be counted he signed Charter 77 and sacrificed his position at Charles University. Six years on, he was a manual labourer by day; at night, and in his spare time, he was organising a team to translate English books for publication in *samizdat*.

We sat round the Kučeras' table drinking coffee in the dark, low-ceilinged room, casting shadows and pockets of light like figures in a Caravaggio painting, whispering or writing notes to each other on scraps of paper so as to avoid mentioning places, names and dates. Money had to be disbursed, book lists drawn up and applications for stipends reviewed. Progress was desperately laboured. As we reached our decisions I slipped the coded details into the inner lining of my bag.

The group around the table now began to talk with increasing animation. Their interests evidently went well beyond philosophy and politics. They wanted to rediscover Bohemia's role in European history and reclaim the national past from the distorted form in which it was conveyed in schools and universities. Pithart's most ambitious project, started in 1977, was the creation of a *samizdat* digest of Czech history, beginning with the rise of eighteenth-century romantic nationalism and ending with the Communist take-over. It was to be an exercise in 'anamnesis', or reversing the obliteration of the past, and it would focus less on dates and events than on the ebb and flow of the language and the evolution of ideas.

Despite his lack of money and freedom, Pithart's professionalism made an impressive contrast to the Marxist methods of Charles University, to which the London School of East European and Slavonic Studies had allied itself. Two historians from Brno and one from Prague (deliberately kept unknown to us) were collecting information, reading source material and gaining access to private archives. Once a fortnight they met to compare notes. At intervals one of them would present a draft chapter for discussion, leading to a revised version, which would be submitted to referees for their comments. The team, Pithart told us, would carry on whether or not we were able to renew our financial assistance, but he made the point that the project had made slow headway until our first instalment of £1,000 had enabled them to employ research assistants and typists. We volunteered to help find foreign referees and contributors and promised to put the grant renewal on the agenda for our next trustees' meeting.

I had had almost nothing to eat and the arrival of wine and tinned mayonnaise salad on tiny squares of buttered bread did little to help. There was still much to get through before Roger's talk and I was beginning to flag. As the hour of the seminar drew near more and more people appeared in the Kučeras' flat, none of whom spoke English. I got by in French and German, with some help from Roger's beginner's Czech, until I was rescued by the arrival of a very tall red-haired woman speaking impeccable English. This was Alena Hromádková, one of the very few women to take an active dissident role, who was here to interpret for Roger. Alena was amusing, easily amused and bursting with vitality. With her long neck and electric presence she suggested a beautiful giraffe, alert to everything around her. She was unmarried and reputed not to have much time for women, but if that was true it never came between us. Having no family, she was spared the unending waste of time and energy on queuing for food that filled the lives of most women (indeed, chaotic distribution was believed by many Czechs to be a deliberate stratagem to exhaust the population).

Alena joined Roger in the far corner of the half-lit room. This was the first lecture I had heard Roger give. A church clock chimed somewhere up the hill, but there was no other sound from the cobbled streets and the room was utterly still. All my tiredness had vanished. Step by step Roger led us through Burke's attack on the French Revolution and dissected the nature, motivations and social preconditions of revolution. His technique of periodically shocking his listeners with an unexpected quotation or with some revolutionary thought of his own, while at the same time distilling an argument to its core and stripping it of jargon, was devastatingly effective. It was evident that Alena's translation captured his thoughts perfectly. I enjoyed the act of interpretation. Ideas had space to enter twice, to be absorbed and to establish themselves.

In the crowded room the expressions on people's faces could just be discerned in the gloom. Looking at Kučera, who had been dismissed from the Academy of Sciences eighteen months earlier, and at some of the more recent dissidents, I could see that Burke was a revelation to them. For me, too, in this setting where politics was no academic game but a matter of survival or annihilation, I felt that night that Burke's insights into the interplay of change and continuity, freedom and social order brought me as close to the meaning of political life as it was possible for me to reach.

Some time after midnight Alena and Roger accompanied me back to the Zlatá Husa hotel through dark, empty streets, watched only by scraggy dogs in alleyways. As we walked, Alena answered all my questions, speaking in a fiery monotone with an idiomatic turn of phrase and an arresting mastery of language. She had visited Oxford in 1968, during her student years, and became a friend of the political scientist Stephen Lukes. Immediately after her return to Prague, her world had disintegrated when the Soviet Army moved in. She managed to get a job teaching English, first at Charles University and later at the Ministry of Health. When she signed Charter 77, the authorities ostensibly ignored her for two years; but in 1980, using the excuse of reorganisation, they threw her out. By the end of the year she was attending Hejdánek's seminars, drawn to them not so much by abstract philosophy as by the hope of change. With her beautifully crafted English, she was invariably translator-in-chief when English-speaking lecturers arrived. She was equally at home in other languages. Once when Stephen Lukes was walking through Prague with her, he was temporarily at a loss for a word: 'I always find when I come here and visit you all, what I can only describe as a sort of "*soulagement*" within myself.' 'Oh, yes,' said Alena immediately, 'an *easing of the soul*.'

Now hanging on precariously to her official job – a project on higher training for economists – Alena was keeping extra copies of sensitive data as raw material for *samizdat* at some later date, when she assumed she would be sacked and forced to support herself as a part-time cleaner. Her hilarious descriptions of her day-to-day existence and the environment in which she and her friends worked, lived and breathed were like a black theatrical fantasy, in which absurdity and cruelty were observed with the deadly accuracy of an artist's eye and made to seem in the end equally ridiculous.

Suddenly we had reached the unlit, rather eerie corridor which led into the Zlatá Husa Hotel. Alena lowered her voice. My questions had delayed her imparting her most important

[28]

message in the safety of the open streets. Now was the moment, she said, to spread the Jan Hus work further afield. She had contacts in Brno, the capital city of Moravia, 200 kilometres south-west of Prague, set in the beautiful wild area of mountains and plains between Bohemia and Slovakia. Her approach, she explained, differed from that of most other dissidents. Having a special interest in those who were determined to keep their jobs, but who sympathised with the dissidents' cause – those who lived and worked in the 'grey zone', as it was known – Alena had built up a network of people who trusted her. She had been recruiting from all sorts of professions and was encouraging people to write incognito for *samizdat* on taboo subjects. In this way ordinary Czechs could learn to escape anonymously from the deceit of their daily existence.

Talking even more quickly and with extraordinary fluency, Alena put in a request for stipends for seven people in Brno. One was a composer; another was preparing history tapes for schoolchildren; another, a computer analyst, was trying to establish accurate statistics for mortality and other social phenomena. Alena told us that many of her contacts were extremely anxious about an imminent ecological catastrophe. The Bohemian forests were being poisoned and the rivers in Moravia polluted by uranium. Any candid discussion of the crisis would lead to dismissal, but she knew of an insider with access to the facts who was preparing a secret exposé of an impending official report. Lastly, she told us of the most important of her protégés, Jiří Müller, who published *samizdat* from his back room. He would set up seminars in Brno if one of us could be tempted to that part of the country.

Every building I had been in during the day had been vastly overheated. The Zlatá Husa was no exception. Casting a huge Austro-Hungarian duvet on and off throughout the night I barely slept, my mind teeming with images, conversations, emotions. I wanted to store every detail in my mind.

Four

Walking quite fast from meeting to meeting in the all but empty streets of Prague, I soon formed the habit of memorising the features of certain passers-by. I had already started to notice the difference between the ordinary inhabitants of the city and those others, more assured, more alert and better shod, who were working for the authorities. I learned to keep watch through the corner of my eye and to turn unexpectedly to face a possible follower.

Petr Rezek, with whom Roger and I had an 'appointment' one particular morning – that is, we had suggested a time in a coded postcard which might or might not have arrived – lived in a pre-war block of flats in the Smíchov district of north-west Prague, on a hill overlooking the city. We planned to travel by tram and walk the last half mile. But as we were about to board, I saw, without looking straight at him, a man in a black leather jacket and jeans standing a few places behind us in the queue. I had seen the same man earlier in the town centre – I recognised him from his sleekness and his buff suede shoes – and knew immediately that he had been observing us.

I flashed a warning look to Roger, but we had rehearsed for this turn of events and had no need for consultation. After two stops I got off at the central intersection. With a casual wave, we parted company and I made for the National Gallery. If we could shake off the secret policeman, we would meet two hours later at Rezek's apartment. I spent long enough admiring the Holbein and the Impressionist room to establish the genuineness of my interest and reached Rezek's flat five minutes after Roger, to find that he too had eluded our follower.

Rezek had a reputation among our trustees for occasional

[30]

charm offset by a violent temper and unpredictable mood swings. Ralph Walker found him so temperamental that before going to see him he would always take the precaution of checking whether it was 'a good day'. His private life was said to be a shambles. I had heard that sessions with him tended to be devoted as much to therapy as to the business in hand. He met me at the door with a troubled air and angry eyes. His saturnine features and wiry, slight figure were tense – this was obviously one of his bad days. Perhaps he was naturally of a nervous disposition; perhaps the years of strain in the underground had been harder for him than for others. In any event, this was my first experience of a dissident who lacked a sense of inner peace. Impatiently, he took the heavy German philosophy books out of the plastic bags that I had been dragging around since I left England, and snatched from Roger's hand a concordance of the Greek philosopher Plotinus. He had been waiting for them for weeks, he said querulously. And where was Kenny's book on Descartes? Where were the political philosophy texts? 'I'm afraid they took them from me at the border,' said Roger apologetically.

For all his idiosyncrasies, Rezek was a serious scholar and a figure of immense importance in the alternative culture. Having lost his job teaching classics, he had attended Hejdánek's seminars for a while, but had fallen out with him. Afterwards, in the utmost secrecy, he had set up a mobile university, giving to a few chosen students an extensive course of lectures, tutorials and seminars on Kant, Aristotle and modern analytical philosophy. Each event took place in a different venue, lent by friends. What made these occasions so dangerous was that Rezek's students, being enrolled at Charles University, still had everything to lose. Discovery would lead to expulsion and a lifetime of surveillance and harassment.

The Trust was Rezek's main external source of books, learned journals and lecturers. Ralph Walker had spoken on Kant, Roger on Aristotle. Before them, the American philosopher Richard Rorty had given a talk, writing in his subsequent report: 'Rezek and Hejdánek are the last functioning humanist intellectuals of a country which once was on even terms with Germany.' He added an afterthought: 'In that situation I too would be alternately suicidal and depressive.'

Roger told Rezek that the trustees had agreed to extend his stipend of £50 a month for another year, and we handed him £150. For a moment he was pleased, but the atmosphere immediately deteriorated when he heard that the Oxford University Press had declined his book on Husserl. Unsuccessfully trying to cushion this blow to his confidence, Roger refrained from mentioning that the two Husserl scholars who had read the text had not found it up to scratch. The scowl deepened. Rezek was seething with suppressed rage. He was producing mountains of work, translating Plotinus, publishing lectures on Homer in the *Musicians' Journal*, writing commentaries on Nietzsche, Wagner and Schopenhauer, and publishing opera criticisms. He now wanted to start his own *samizdat* philosophy journal, he said, giving me a package of sample articles to take back to England. He urgently needed more financial support, which with our meagre funds we could not guarantee to supply.

Not wanting to leave on a sour note, we changed the subject. Rezek was musical (he was especially knowledgeable about opera). Finding we shared his interest in Czech composers, he walked us to the second-hand music shop in Myslíkova Street, a musty ground floor room where every tattered manuscript had been inscribed and annotated fifty or more years ago, leaving posterity with enigmatic hints of life in pre-war Bohemia. Here it was still possible to buy early editions of Smetana, Dvořák and Janáček. Rezek grew calmer as we sifted through a pile of ancient scores. After a while we left him.

Our next rendezvous, set up by Alena, was with the pseudonymous 'Petr Fidelius'. It was not until after the fall of Communism that any of us was told his real name, Karel Palek. The three of us, Alena, Roger and I, met him on a street corner after an exchange of clandestine messages. We started by walking about aimlessly until he was convinced we were not being followed. With his finely-proportioned, sensitive face, his *joie de vivre,* his pointed beard and his black broad-rimmed hat, Palek was the image of the artist in *La Bohème.* He had never worked within the system, having chosen to go underground immediately after graduating in 1972. He counted himself lucky to have obtained a position as a boiler stoker, long before such jobs became the ambition of disgraced teachers. (Nearly all the large buildings in Prague were heated by fifteen-foot-wide steel drums, into which stokers shovelled cheap brown Polish coal, creating a pall of strong-smelling smoke over the city that left one's eyes sealed up with dust after a night's sleep.)

We headed underground into an airless cavity in the cellars of an old hospital. Here Palek introduced us courteously to his territory, which consisted of his boiler and an adjoining space where through an oily light I could just pick out strange objects – an upright piano on which was scattered music from Schubert to the Blues, and an assortment of kitsch photographs, figurines and jewelled flowers. Palek was an authority on kitsch. 'Communist culture', he said, 'is kitsch with teeth.'

In the centre of the partitioned area stood the desk around which his life's work revolved. Our trustees had been worried about the amount of money we were sending to him with little apparent result, but all doubts were swept away as we took in the scope and quality of his activities. He was editor and publisher of *Kritický Sborník,* a journal produced in tiny editions of forty. We were shown the entire sequence – nearly three years of quarterly publications, each of about a hundred pages, containing articles on Czech culture and history, together with memoirs, notes on unobtainable authors, and so on. A unique feature was a summary of the entire corpus of works in *samizdat.*

Palek had also initiated a number of translations and a series of books devoted to the recovery of Czechoslovakia's lost historical memory. We looked at two of these volumes. There was beauty in the large typed lettering hammered out through the black or red ribbons of prehistoric typewriters, in the tracer-thin paper on which the *samizdat* copy was printed, and in the sage-green or brown binding. The crackly pages were redolent of a world in which scholarship mattered because it was an act of defiance, and in which thought had the hand-made quality of the books that contained it. And the covers were nostalgically reminiscent of the faded mauve and grey bus tickets of my 1950s childhood, my pale orange and blue matchbox-top collection and the subdued colours of my stamps.

It was imperative, Palek emphasised, to confine knowledge of his work to our innermost circle. The reason his operation had been able to survive for three years was that his network had never been compromised. When forced to choose between delay and trusting someone whose loyalty was an unknown quantity, he had always chosen caution. As it happened we knew his co-editor, but he did not want us to meet anyone else connected with him. 'Teamwork is dangerous,' he said. Alena judged his situation to be so sensitive that she asked us not to take documents from him but to let her send them through underground channels. He promised to get new publications to us as and when they appeared, but, since his 'print run' consisted of only ten or a dozen carbon copies, he noted ruefully that to do so was to lose a significant percentage of his production.

Palek had also written his own book[1] under his pseudonym of Petr Fidelius, in which he had subjected Orwell's idea of Newspeak to intense scrutiny. He explained the peculiar syntax, vocabulary and rhetoric of Marxist-Leninism by the fact that correspondence of language with human experience had been marginalised. Words had been reduced to no more than an instrument of power.

Once an hour Palek would rise from his seat, take off his velvet jacket and silk neckerchief, put on a pair of overalls and with a faint smile descend the two steps into the boiler house.

[1] It had just been published in Munich. It would be published in Paris three years later as *L'esprit post-totalitaire*.

He concluded our visit with a performance of Scott Joplin. Fired by a strong cup of coffee and the vibrant music, Alena, Roger and I danced compulsively on the upper tier to the beat of the honky tonk. I shall not forget the sight of that elegant Central European figure drumming out ragtime tunes with abandoned insouciance, among piles of books and illicit manuscripts, careless, just for a moment, of the fatal knock on the door.

Our next call was to Radim Palouš, who had just ended his term as a Charter 77 spokesman to resume his life as an underground writer. Roger and I walked down to the south bank of the River Vltava and knocked on the side door of an ancient mill. A solid-looking man of medium height opened the door. He had intelligent eyes and an indefinable air of civilisation about him. This was Palouš.

Having seen the plain interiors of dissidents' living quarters a few times, I was struck that they nearly all had the same atmosphere. There would be a solid desk, a chair and a good reading lamp: the spare and ordered rooms of an academic. The books on the shelves would be wrapped for protection the way that I had been taught to wrap them as a child after the war, in thick grey or brown paper, the flaps folded over into sharp triangles. But if I now expected the familiar austere surroundings, I was in for a surprise. Without a word, Palouš took us into a panelled room with worn leather chairs, dark brass objects and knobbled books bound in maroon leather stamped with gold lettering – his family's original library, a collection of eighteenth-and nineteenth-century books from imperial times. The room had the private serenity of a scholar's study, but it had been violated by intruders at some stage, for there was no corner where it was safe to talk. 'This place is infested with bugs. They're everywhere, every floor, every wall, every switch' he said, unlocking a drawer in his desk and taking out a package. We followed him out to the front of the mill house, across the flagstones to a wooden bench, in full view of the pedestrians who streamed across the Charles Bridge not a hundred yards away.

There was not much point in secrecy. Charter spokesmen were marked men. In any case, Palouš's relaxed, unhurried manner was infectious and I soon became oblivious to our surroundings. We sat for an hour in the noonday sun, listening absorbed as he took us through his essays. He handed us three manuscripts for possible publication in the West. He had also completed a more substantial book on the philosopher Jan Patočka, which would appear in *samizdat* as soon as he was able to pay for the typing. In anticipation of the assent of our fellow trustees, we gave him an advance of £50. He needed three times as much to see the book through, but it was all we could afford.

The name of Patočka had cropped up over and over again during my stay in Czechoslovakia. Such was his hold on the imagination of the dissidents that some of the younger ones had suggested at Roger's lecture that I might take flowers to his grave, which lay in a cemetery near the Břevnov monastery on the western edge of Prague.

After the all too familiar round of exclusion, rehabilitation and purge, Patočka had effectively created the underground university through his secret seminars, in which he developed his philosophical and political theories into a coherent pattern. To Patočka the catastrophe of the modern world was the notion of a society in which people are to be valued only as instruments for a larger purpose – and worst of all, as instruments for the pseudo-scientific goals of the totalitarian state. What gave him his special resonance among the dissidents was his exploration of the moralities of everyday life, based on the need to accept personal responsibility. So influential were his seminars that they were to be acknowledged by Václav Havel, Palouš and others as the fundamental basis for adopting the 'alternative life' and rejecting the evasions on which the Communist state apparatus relied.

As a founder spokesman of Charter 77, Patočka had been the regime's public enemy number one. Arrested in 1978, he suffered a fatal cerebral haemorrhage during a brutal interrogation. After his death, Palouš took over his seminars and began the task of editing his papers, none of which had been published in his native land. The forthcoming book would be Palouš's tribute to his friend and mentor, and to a life lived in truth.

During the last few days I had not thought twice about accepting *samizdat* material and had stuffed my small suitcase with manuscripts. But when I reached the airport I was annoyed to find myself in a state of high anxiety. Carrying English and American philosophy books from London to Prague had been relatively easy. Taking papers out, written in a language I could not pretend to know, was quite another thing. A sinister-looking customs official loomed nearer. I had memorised or encoded names, addresses and appointments, so I knew I could cause our Czech contacts little harm unless information was extracted from me by methods too hideous to contemplate. For a split second the grey-uniformed figure stared at me. Then he casually stamped my bags and I was through. For the next six years, that was how I travelled in and out of Eastern Europe – with hand luggage and a tourist visa. And, with one exception, I escaped being caught.

Five

I had also a private motive for helping the Czech dissidents. I needed distraction from some shattering news at home.

About a year before becoming editor of *The Times,* Charlie had suffered acute back pain, initially attributed to a slipped disc. However, at Easter 1983, when he fell and broke his leg, the hospital consultants embarked on an ominously elaborate series of tests. The diagnosis was bone cancer. We were told that his expectation of survival could be up to ten years, but that the prospects were improving all the time with the progress of research. He toyed with the idea of alternative medicine, but ruled it out, if only because it would have entailed long stays in a clinic and he had no intention of taking time off work. That left him with the conventional forms of treatment, radiation and chemotherapy. So as to go on living as normal life as possible, we decided to keep his condition secret. In spite of painful fractures of the bones in his arms and legs he continued editing and writing as though nothing had happened, explaining away his intermittent hospitalisation as due to complications arising from an old riding accident.

A month after my visit to Prague I became a trustee of the Jan Hus. We met every two or three months, sometimes in Oxford in the rooms of the philosopher Stuart Hampshire, sometimes in London at Roger Scruton's flat. There was plenty of work to contend with – journalists to supply with stories, funds to raise, expeditions to prepare, *samizdat* to read and translate. Before each mission we would brief the lecturer on safety precautions and issue instructions to memorise or encode. It was a strict part of our routine that the debriefing on return should be based on written reports. Cumulatively, these

were in the end to provide a unique portrait of the underground world and its enemies.

From the late autumn of 1983 we piloted a succession of
academics into Czechoslovakia to give lectures and to take in
books, journals, money and equipment for printing and publishing. They found a darkening atmosphere. When the Oxford
philosopher Christopher Kirwan returned from giving a seminar on Augustine, his report noted that Hejdánek's last two
Monday meetings had been broken up and 'everyone detained
for questioning'.

The air of tension resulted from a recent change of political
tack. Brezhnev and Andropov had staked heavily on *détente*,
with the aim of seducing NATO not to deploy nuclear missiles in
Europe. The advent of Reagan and Thatcher signalled a setback
to that strategy, and the Soviet stance now became highly aggressive. The world, they implied, was on a knife edge. Provocation
by the United States might at any time justify the USSR in launch-
ing a pre-emptive nuclear strike. Taking their cue from Moscow,
the Czech authorities, too, had switched to a harder line. There
was no longer the same incentive to be soft on dissidents.

Robert Grant, who taught English Literature at Glasgow
University and had offered to buy the dissidents a word-
processor out of his own pocket, found them bearing up well
under their harassment:

They said with due gratitude that, if discovered, any such
hardware could land them in the soup. It was then that I
realised that what they already do goes on more or less with
the full knowledge of the authorities, and that this quasi tol-
erance amounts to a bizarre and unremitting system of control and repression, a sort of cat-and-mouse game. The
cheerfulness and high morale of these people, their vehement
but completely unpriggish consciousness of right and
decency, were very striking... I should mention that there
was something of a crackdown afoot. I heard next day that
Alena H. had been followed after leaving us on the metro,

and apparently we had been followed to Kučera's on Friday... Pithart, whom I was supposed to meet the next day, was lying low in the country and did not want to risk coming to Prague...

He was profoundly impressed by the calibre of his audience.

The talk I gave was some more or less impromptu reflections on the relations between state and civil society...My audience was sharp and critical. One of them, Václav Benda, had come out at considerable risk, since he is under constant surveillance. Bratinka translated in long paragraphs. He seemed – as they all did – completely familiar with the kind of thing I was saying (which was strange, considering how utterly *outré* such things are in the UK, even in the politics department). I came in for a lot of flak, Benda in particular going straight to the main weakness. Clearly my audience were in fundamental sympathy with the ideas that I was floating off, but they wanted a lot greater coherence than I provided.

They had little time for the small print in moral and political issues, not because they were bigots and wished to ignore it, but because, in their endless intellectual leisure and under the continual pressure of events, they had acquainted themselves with it all and sorted the dross from the ore. I could not help thinking what a feeble lot, intellectually speaking, our own professional political philosophers are, even the great names in contemporary academia. The reason is that, to them, none of it really *matters*. These people were, despite the comparative provinciality of outlook natural to their unfortunate position, immensely more intelligent, critical and cultivated than their opposite numbers here.

Robert Grant had put his finger on the spot. Our lecturers went out to teach, but it was they, rather than their listeners, who were the more enriched by the experience.

As my admiration for the dissidents grew, so did my frustration at the indifference of the British establishment. The Czech desk at the Foreign Office met us with condescending nods that told us better than words that we were no more than a potentially embarrassing nuisance to them. The Church of England ignored all our appeals. As for the universities, with the exception of a few individuals, they not only ignored the dissidents but fêted their persecutors, showering lightweights from Charles University with lecture invitations while scholars who would have shone in any senior common room in the world were enduring a catacomb existence in the cellars of Prague.

The quality of *samizdat* output was, of course, uneven. The separation of the wheat from the chaff would have made a fascinating exercise for the School of East European and Slavonic Studies at London University. The faculty there, however, took at face value the fiction that there were no banned Czech authors and refused to take *samizdat* seriously, dismissing it as the product of marginalised political activists whose literary or intellectual talents were overrated because of the hardship of the life they had chosen.

The attitude of the intellectual élite seemed to stem not only from a general mistrust of ideas, emanating elsewhere than from the left, but also from awe of Moscow. Perhaps there was something about the USSR's sheer size, its military strength and its closed society that produced a suspension of critical faculties. Whatever the explanation, while Reagan and Thatcher were incurring something akin to hatred among Western liberals, Yuri Andropov, former head of the KGB, found himself the improbable recipient of the sympathy – or at least the acquiescence – of half the European academic world.

At this time of deep division, *The Times* under Charlie knew where it stood.

Much Western commentary reveals a curious double standard which accepts that it is unexceptionable when Soviet rhetoric is challenging and aggressive but wrong when the West replies in kind. The Soviet leadership has shown since the Russian Revolution that what it cannot achieve openly, it will try to achieve by subversion, propaganda or just plain intimidation... The period of deténte came to be seen in the West as a suspension of hostilities, while the Soviet leadership never made any secret of the fact that the conflict between the systems was to continue, but by other means.

Charlie marked the advent of the New Year with a leader on George Orwell's *Nineteen Eighty-Four* and the demoralising effect of the appropriation of the language by the State – the same message that Karel Palek had voiced to me in his boilerhouse in Prague. No greater tribute could be paid to Orwell than the risks the dissidents took to make *Nineteen Eighty-Four* available to their compatriots. Smuggled in from the West, copied out by hand or reproduced in clandestine publications – in typescript in Czechoslovakia and Hungary, and in printed and even illustrated versions in Poland – the book, if discovered, invariably attracted a heavy prison sentence. A British Library exhibition I went to that year put on display early *samizdat* editions in no less than eleven different languages.

For some months after his initial dose of drugs Charlie's condition had remained stable, but in February he broke his left arm for the second time. Soon afterwards he broke three ribs. Another round of radiation and chemotherapy was prescribed. Somehow he summoned up the strength and courage to overcome his exhausting treatment, never missing a day in the office. He refused to be disheartened, as if willing people to ignore the mutilating side effects. His incapacitation seemed if anything to add to his authority, as he poured out a series of leaders on every subject under the sun.

It was an unspoken pact between us that we would not accept signs that his health was deteriorating, but would continue as if nothing much was amiss. The strain of internalising our situation came out in my painting. In a premonition of Charlie's ordeal, I had once painted a series of crucifixions. Now, still obsessed by pain, I turned to different themes – to street scenes and interiors in Prague, in which lone figures contemplated in dark rooms, or walked the streets, or kneeled in supplication outside church doorways. The sense of isolation, prayer and redemption was for all of us – for Charlie, for my sons, for the dissidents, not least for myself.

I had heard a good deal about Pavel Bratinka from other visitors. I knew, for example, that he was a Catholic convert and that he had abandoned a promising career as a physicist to become a founder of Charter 77. As chance would have it, however, our paths did not cross until my third visit in October 1984.

Bratinka supported his wife and four children by stoking boilers on the ground floor of a featureless concrete building on a derelict site near the Powder Tower, the ancient gate in Náměsti Republiky between the old town of Prague and the new. I picked my way there past a wasteland of broken bricks and fractured timber, uncomfortably conspicuous in the foreign cut of my tweed coat. An old, hunched woman crept out of Jakubová Street. Otherwise there was no one. I eventually found Bratinka in a little chamber situated just off the area where the vast silent steel cylinders stood.

He was seated at a wooden table, above him a single crucifix and a couple of shelves holding books – among them Justinian's Roman Civil Law, the Jowett edition of Plato's *Dialogues* and some of Thomas Aquinas's Commentaries. After our initial handshake, he returned to the open volume of Plato that he had been reading when I arrived, giving me the chance to study his face as he recited a passage in which Socrates argues that nobody should accept authority over his fellow citizens without having demonstrated a sustainable capacity to resist both pleasure and fear. Socrates' words seemed to come across to him with the immediacy of a personal message from the father of Western philosophy.

He had the appearance of a man in his late thirties. His soft, smooth skin was strangely incongruous with his strong face and confident voice – let alone his rough surroundings. During our talk he hardly ever looked directly at me and I had long opportunities to consider the profile of his nose, which was like that of an emperor on a Roman coin, aquiline with a bump half way down. Having learned his English through books and learned journals, he spoke in faultless sentences, salting faintly archaic and poetic expressions with Central European wit and learning.

Everything he set his mind to had a purpose. He had joined forces with his friend and fellow Catholic, the mathematician Václav Benda, to persuade the Church to identify religion with overt opposition to Communism. Needing a legal framework for their crusade as well as a moral one, Bratinka had taught himself law in the American Embassy library. The basis of their case was Czechoslovakia's international obligation to respect civil rights, reflected in its signature of the Helsinki Accords.

Considering the impact of Solidarity in Poland I wondered why the Catholic Church in Czechoslovakia had not been equally effective. 'Have patience,' said Bratinka, 'it will be.' The leadership, he told me, had been destroyed in the 1950s, when many priests had been tortured, killed or herded into concentration camps. Their congregations, too, had suffered cruel harassment. Hopes of revival were stirred by the Prague Spring but crushed again after 1968, when the Government shut down most of the few remaining churches and seminaries. For a brief while a handful of Catholics in Brno and Olomouc had carried on, but they, too, were soon subdued by a further round of arrests. Bratinka brought the gruesome story to life in richly detailed narrative.

The proclamation of a Polish pope in 1978 had brought repercussions almost as resounding in Czechoslovakia as in Poland. In 1982 the Vatican barred priests from membership of political organisations, a decree directed at *Pacem in Terris,* which had operated as a Marxist front within the Czech Church for years. This marked a turning point. The 84-year-old Patriarch, Cardinal Tomášek, who hitherto had acted as a puppet leader, regained his courage and quashed a revolt against the Vatican ban. 'The authorities were not so fortunate,' Bratinka said, enjoying the irony of the situation. 'They believed – and who could blame them, after so many years? – that they were dealing with a weakling, whom they could manipulate as they pleased, but they found instead a Thomas à Becket, and no convenient way to rid themselves of this "turbulent priest".'

With the excommunication of *Pacem in Terris*, the door was ajar for clandestine Catholics to rejoin the Church openly. Bratinka put at over 500 the number of priests who had been celebrating mass secretly in their homes, at great risk to their lives. At least 100 more were undergoing prison sentences. Sooner rather than later all these would return to the fold. It was a sign of the times that some of the excommunicated collaborators had recanted and had been accepted back into the Church. Bratinka was convinced that the religious groundswell was strong enough to be the making of a real threat to the regime.

Where Bratinka was unusual among Czech intellectuals was in his mastery of liberal and conservative ideas. He was well read in de Tocqueville, Burke and Popper and had been persuaded by Hayek, whose *Road to Serfdom* he was translating, that the paramount aim of society should be the liberty of the individual within the rule of law. He tuned in regularly to the BBC World Service and was an avid reader of the international press in the libraries of the American Embassy and the British Council.

I was envious of his working day: of its peacefulness and the absence of the electrical paraphernalia on which so much of twentieth-century Western life depended but which suddenly appeared to me ridiculous. To open the boiler doors, to rake the cinders and to shovel in lumps of coal seemed in his presence an entirely satisfying activity, a routine that served to encourage creativity, not to dull it.

As I walked away from his monk-like cell, back across the rubble into the empty streets, I reflected how the brevity of our meeting and the suspense generated by its enforced secrecy had intensified communication between us. There was no gossip or small talk. He had swept straight into the centre of the human condition, as if this were the most natural thing in the world. There had been an instant rapport between us, yet whether from courtesy or shyness, or from his absorption in his many tasks at hand, he asked no intimate questions of me – how I lived and worked in England. Whatever the reason, I was grateful. Safe from personal intrusion, I did not have to find words for my own developing tragedy at home. More than any of the dissidents, it was Bratinka who was to lead me beyond my own familiar world, and if I was eventually to disappoint him by not turning Catholic, I came to have the utmost respect for his faith and his integrity – indeed for everything he stood for. His strength and self-containment was contagious. My anxiety over Charlie never left me; but it was quietened when I was with Bratinka.

Six

What I saw of Czechoslovakia made me curious about life in the other Soviet satellite states. I was sure that dissident philosophers and artists in Poland, Hungary and elsewhere were being persecuted, but I wondered what form their persecution took: whether they were managing to keep abreast of their subjects, whether they, too, were in need of books, journals and a new line of contact with the West.

That I chose Poland first was partly due to Bratinka, who had urged me to go there to see the country for myself and to bring him an account of the current state of the Catholic Church. Polish academics could travel without much difficulty to the West. Many came to the North Oxford house of Leszek Kolakowski, who had abandoned Communism while professor at the University of Warsaw and whose monumental work, *Main Currents of Marxism*, was generally considered the most powerful analysis of the subject ever written. Among the train of pilgrims to the Kolakowskis' sitting room one especially caught my attention – Marcin Król, a Catholic historian.

Król had recently published in the official Polish press a study of nineteenth-century conservative thought. He was also a sort of licensed underground editor. His semi-*samizdat* journal, *Res Publica,* explored in a theoretical manner such counter-revolutionary concepts as the integrity of private property and the supremacy of the rule of law over the state. Tall, sophisticated and intense, with a mild air of disdain, he had the alluring, chain-smoking aura of the Parisian Left Bank. He asked me to bring him the latest issues of *Encounter* if I ever came to Warsaw, and I promised I would.

My actual departure was triggered by a chance reading of an

article in the *Sunday Telegraph* by the Catholic journalist Mary Kenny. She wrote mainly about the threatened Polish Church. But she ended with an unusual message: would anyone from the British theatre accept an invitation to participate in a forthcoming symposium at Poznań? If so, they were to contact a Mrs Irina Slawinska. Accommodation and meals would be provided. No doubt the request was aimed at actors and directors, but who cared? Using my credentials as a costume designer for the National Theatre, I wrote off immediately in my maiden name of Gwynne .

My expectations were high. I saw Poland as the most tragic and most heroic of countries. Its fate during the war, when its Jewish population was sent to the concentration camps and the Russian Army stood idle at the gates to allow the Nazis to massacre the heroes of the Warsaw uprising, made it a symbol of the horrors of the twentieth century. Nevertheless, after the war it had escaped the worst features of Stalinism. Its Communist Party was not purged, nor was its agriculture collectivised, nor the Church subjugated. Early in 1981 the world had watched mesmerised as Solidarity, led by the steelworker Lech Wałęsa, competed for authority with the Party. Over a period of a year the Government had been obliged to agree to widespread reform; large parts of the state administration had broken down. During its final months, after recruiting 10 million workers, peasants and intellectuals, Solidarity's aim was to end Communism through a peaceful evolutionary process. A worker from Poznań called it 'a revolution of the soul'. The people felt able at last to speak their minds openly in the workplace as well as behind closed doors at home. They were no longer prepared to live double lives.

Then, in December 1981, the military and police arms of the Government had moved in. Solidarity's activists were imprisoned, censorship was reintroduced and arbitrary arrest became common. Although the orders had come ostensibly from the Polish authorities, it was no secret that the posters announcing the imposition of martial law had been printed in the USSR. Yet ferocious though the clampdown was, Solidarity was not alto-gether crushed. Many of its leaders retained a following in the West long after they had been driven underground. Adam Michnik, for example, who had founded the Committee for the Protection of Workers, the intellectual wing of Solidarity, con-tinued to smuggle articles out of prison which Charlie regularly published in the *The Times*.

I arrived in Warsaw at the end of February 1984, the coldest time of the year, taking with me Norman Davies's history of Poland, *The Heart of Europe*, and a few other innocent enough books and magazines. Depositing most of my belongings in the flat of Roger Boyes, the *Times* correspondent in Warsaw, I set off to buy my train ticket. On the way to the station, as a mark of respect to Father Popiełuszko, a priest about whom I had been reading in the *Herald Tribune*, I visited St Stanisław Kostka Church. The pews were filled with praying figures even on a weekday in the middle of the morning. I then caught the train to Poznań. My compartment was full of shabby drunks, one of whom snoozed unsuccessfully on my unwelcoming shoulder, while his poor humiliated little boy in the seat oppo-site tried to pretend it was not his father. The outlook from my carriage window, during the six-hour journey, was fog-grey, depressing and chill. I had an address, but no other instructions how to reach my destination.

Poznań had escaped the massive bombing of Warsaw and at first it was reassuring to walk among its untouched nineteenth-century buildings. But police and military were everywhere – not overtly, but lurking in passages and alleyways off the main streets. Any official I spoke to stared with hostility and suspi-cion, or gave me the 'glass eye' look. An air of tension emanated from passers-by. No. 2 Wieszawa Street turned out to be a seminary for Jesuit priests. I rang an echoing bell until the heavy wooden door was opened by a white-faced young man in a dark cassock. I pointed to the name of Irina Slawinska on my piece of paper. He led me immediately to a small study where an elderly woman was sitting. 'You are very brave,' she said. 'I did not think you would get here.' In truth I was not so much brave as exhausted by my first exposure to Polish existence, queuing for hours for a ticket nobody wanted to sell me, sitting in a long-delayed unheated train, and trying to find my way without a map in a town without taxis. The problem was compounded by the knowledge that any telephone call would be tapped.

Irina Slawinska's warmth and friendliness were like an oasis. Even if all else went wrong, now at least I would learn something of the true Poland. A religious teacher at the University of Lublin for more than twenty-five years, she had been a colleague there of Karól Wojtyła, who at that time was Bishop of Cracow and was later to become the Pope. Lublin was the only autonomous university in Eastern Europe – it was financed by the Vatican and linked with an independent publishing house in Cracow called Znak. Znak was allowed to print virtually any scholarly or academic text, although since the imposition of martial law a few authors, including Orwell and Solzhenitsyn, had been proscribed.

Two gentle priests gave me a programme and escorted me into the nearby hall. They interpreted for me in turn, one in English, the other in French. In my seat of honour in the front row, I found myself alone among 300 black-robed figures who were listening to a talk by Poland's foremost actress, Maja Komoronska. She spoke of her involvement with Solidarity, of the love of mother and son, of the poems she would read, and of the Polish theatre. Then it was question time: what advice could Madame Komoronska give a priest for his diction during mass? 'You can do no better than follow the Pope's way of speaking, especially his pauses ...'

Irina Slawinska's contribution was an hour-long lecture with theological and philosophical reflections on the theatre. How do plays truly touch people? How can they portray a picture of what man is, if only God knows the truth in man? Then the priest who was organising the conference addressed me from the stage in English, thanking 'Jessica Gwynne from the

National Theatre, London, for coming from England', adding, as if I were from another planet, how surprised they all were to see me. And indeed I might have been from another planet. The idea of a religious symposium on drama conducted before several hundred priests would have seemed utterly bizarre in London or New York.

Back in Irina Slawinska's study, I asked whether the authorities knew what was going on at the conference. Yes, there would be a bugging system in the hall, but probably not here, where we were sitting. By now I had been assigned a third interpreter, this time a German-speaker. As we walked round the seminary, the priests described in hushed voices the nature of life in Poland. They told me of the lack of food and ordinary necessities such as lavatory paper and light bulbs; how nearly everything was stolen before reaching the shops; how the Party controlled the key appointments – business managers, publishers, newspaper editors, judges, trade union leaders, university rectors, headmasters, bankers – every position that mattered in every walk of life. Failure to be endorsed by the Party prevented even the most talented from holding a creative job in the theatre. The slightest exercise of initiative could lead to denunciation or imprisonment.

The recent leadership changes in Moscow confirmed their worst fears for Poland's future. Andropov had died a week or two before my visit to Poznań, and had been succeeded by an old-guard *apparatchik* from the Brezhnev era, Konstantin Chernenko, in whose youthful history there lurked unpleasant shadows. The new Soviet leader had earned his political spurs in the NKVD, the forerunner of the KGB, which had been responsible for the purges of 'undesirables' and 'class enemies' during the post-First World War Russian terror. Chernenko was a particularly close comrade of Miroslaw Milewski, the head of Security Affairs in the Warsaw politburo.

In the evening my three priests took me to a tenth-century church in the centre of Poznań to see T. S. Eliot's *Murder in The Cathedral*. Crowds packed the pews, aisle and gangway to overflowing. The production was a barely concealed symbolic depiction of the Polish spiritual condition. The Devil's temptation of Thomas à Becket held the audience transfixed. At the moment of his murder, loud triumphant music rang through the church. In the last scene the producer had inserted his own text: three actors dressed as soldiers strode to the footlights and spouted satire on Polish life, mocking state television programmes and miming attempts by the police to prevent groups conspiring at street corners. (A few months later, in Wrocław, I was to see a production before a similarly packed audience of Albert Camus's *La Peste,* in which Camus's rats were dressed as Party hacks with long creepy tails doubling as police batons.)

News soon spread that I was a visitor from England. Five people came up to me separately and pressed flimsy packages into my hands, wrapped in thin envelopes. Inside, they whispered, were articles describing the situation in Poland. Would I take them, to give to any newspaper of my choice when I returned to England? I slipped them all into my bag.

It was very late when I was taken to the apartment of the German-speaking priest's sister, where I was to spend the night on her sofa. She had three tiny rooms for a family of four. In the sitting-room the son, aged eight, was in preparation for his first communion. We kneeled at a makeshift altar with two lit candles on either side of the icon dedicated to the Black Madonna, whose shrine stood at Jasna Góra in Częstochowa. I wrote in my diary.'The priest prayed in song for a quarter of an hour while I just kneeled. Then his sister brought us tea and home-made bottled blackcurrants which we spooned into the tea. It was the first non-processed food I had seen since I had been in Poland.'

The priests helped me to hire a car in Poznań and I made a long detour back to Warsaw. The gloom of my first few hours had long since evaporated. Poland to me now seemed rich and vivid. Everywhere were straight fields and tall birch trees, the only colour the flame of the sun in icy ponds and ditches. It was a nineteenth-century landscape. In the fields thickly padded peasants were mending carts and ploughs and feeding the farm animals with root vegetables. They travelled the roads by horse and trailer. In the towns, hideous post-war concrete architecture housed the inhabitants in battery farm conditions; Stalinist industrial plants engulfed everything with visible and invisible pollution, despoiling districts where once had stood ancient buildings and humiliating what little beauty remained by the aggressive juxtaposition of ugliness. To the west of the historic city of Cracow, the huge post-war iron-smelting factories of Nowa Huta sprawled over hundreds of acres, belching out clouds of sulphur dioxide which ate into the stonework of the eighteenth-century buildings in the city centre.

Away from the main cities in the countryside I came to understand the binding effect of the Catholic Church in Poland. At hundreds of street corners lighted candles flickered beneath statuettes of Christ or the Virgin Mary in narrow shrines carved into the walls or free-standing, like small stone temples, five or six foot high. In every town or village the church was the focal point, holding several masses a week. I stopped frequently to enter them. A sense of redemption and renewal through suffering pervaded every congregation. For millions of Polish men and women Catholicism was not only their comfort but also their means of unshackling the mind from state ideology.

More than anyone, though, it was Father Popiełuszko who kept the population from despair. One month after martial law, when death was the penalty for anti-state pronouncements and dismissal or imprisonment for being linked to Solidarity, Father Popiełuszko gave the first of what became known as his 'Masses for the Country'. On the last Sunday evening of each month in St Stanisław Kostka Church in north Warsaw he said a prayer, followed by a three-minute silence, for all those in distress from the effects of martial law. The authorities had begun to threaten him with reprisals if he continued. His

Masses for the Country were now copied in churches throughout Poland.

On reaching Warsaw I went straight to the home of Marcin
Król, bringing with me the copies of *Encounter* I had promised
him at the Kolakowskis' in Oxford. It was my first meeting
with his wife, the beautiful Małgorzata, a woman of excep-
tional elegance, with classic high cheekbones. I was completely
charmed by her. She specialised in directing little known early
operas and we hatched a plan to invite British singers to
Warsaw to perform in her productions based on librettos
obtained by me in London. I would also design some of her
sets.

I could see from the stacked copies in his study of Marcin's
monthly journal *Res Publica* that he expected a wide range
of interest from his readers. He ran articles on law, history,
literature and philosophy. A recent piece was on a subject particularly sensitive to the Poles with their own record of anti-
Semitism – Jewish culture and its place in the Polish experience.
An article by Marcin himself discussed the meaning of 'the
Right' in the context of modern Polish politics. Few in Poland
in the early '80s had access to liberal economic ideas. Solidarity's programme, still in an early stage of formation, had been
drawn from a spectrum of traditions, calling for such universal
values as freedom, democracy and the rule of law, but in political and economic terms it was unsure whether to espouse
socialist reform, a radical move to free markets or some inter-
mediate position.

What Marcin showed me highlighted a telling difference
between the Czech and Polish predicaments. Thanks to the
legacy of Solidarity, photocopying machines were in abundant
supply in Poland, where journals were able to sustain print
runs of up to 10,000 copies, in contrast to the wretched twelve
copies of Kučera's *Střední Evropa* in Prague. The distinction
between *samizdat* and officially sanctioned publications was
therefore quite blurred in Poland. Academic articles could, as a
rule, be published freely. Marcin could write far more openly

than any Czech writer about Patočka – even about the circumstances of his death under interrogation. Beyond a certain limit, however, the oppression was the same. To oppose the military regime, to reveal the extent of arbitrary arrest and maltreatment, was just as much a prisonable offence in Poland as it would have been in any other Iron Curtain country.

On the Sunday evening I joined a vast congregation of worshippers at Father Popiełuszko's mass. He spoke of the long history of Poland's sufferings and of the way that the Catholic faith had given their forebears courage to keep alive the hope for a free and Christian country. One of Poland's leading actors recited passages chosen by Popiełuszko from the works of Polish poets and thinkers. The atmosphere in the church was charged with faith, but also with tension, for not everyone was there for religious inspiration. Some at the back, clad in leather jackets and jeans, lurked by the doors to identify faces and to observe the message of the sermon.

Next day I took the plane to London. What I had seen had fascinated and saddened me in ways that I could not have explained except to one who had been through similar experiences. I showed my report to Roger Scruton who had been to Poland the previous year. After comparing notes, we decided to set up a Polish trust along the lines of the Jan Hus, but concentrating less on philosophy than on the theatre, the Church, medicine, music and literature. We named it the Jagiellonian Foundation after Poland's thirteenth-century royal family, kings of Lithuania after whom the university in Cracow had been named. We selected twelve patrons and five working trustees, from among whom we persuaded Caroline Cox, recently elevated to the House of Lords for her work in education, to act as chairman.

The Polish secret police were more efficient than their Czech counterparts. Nonetheless, their methods of preventing us from 'conspiring against the ideals of socialism' were paradoxical. An article in the newspaper Życie Warszawy gave an uncannily accurate account of our missions and reported Government statements to the effect that anyone engaging in such activities would be subject to the severest penalties – not excluding the death penalty. Yet they waited a year before taking me in for interrogation. Roger Scruton and Caroline Cox, both of whom travelled to Poland several times a year (Caroline taking in trucks of medical supplies), were never arrested.

Looking back now over our yellowing xeroxed reports, some handwritten, but most typed on antiquated typewriters, it is reassuring to be reminded how many visitors and books and how much printing and medical equipment we were able to ferry into Poland. But in truth our contribution in those fields was matched by numerous others. Where we made our strongest impact was over the tragedy that was to befall Father Popiełuszko.

Seven

On 3 March 1984, the day after my return from Poland, Charlie and I were among the guests of the Home Secretary, Willie Whitelaw, at a formal dinner at Dorneywood, a Government-owned country house made available to Cabinet ministers. Mrs Thatcher was to be there, and I hoped to have a chance to pass a message to her about the mood in Eastern Europe.

Unfortunately others were claiming Mrs Thatcher's attention with their own agendas. In any case, having just returned from Andropov's funeral in Moscow, what she really wanted to talk about was the USSR. She had gone chiefly to obtain an impression of the new Soviet leader, Chernenko. He was old and ill. His speech was stumbling and in the open air he had behaved oddly, seeming unable to breathe – although once indoors he had soon recovered. 'He won't last long,' she said. By the end of the evening I had still not found an opportunity to speak to her.

Next day I steeled myself to write her a letter. I told her of the strength of the Polish opposition and of their admiration for her as a symbol of hope. After her high-profile visit to Hungary three weeks earlier – her first to a Warsaw Pact country – there was widespread concern that she might have been taken in by Prime Minister Kadar's 'liberalisation programme' and might be planning to soften her approach toward the Soviet bloc. Her hand-written reply was as robust as the most courageous dissident could have hoped: 'I have been a little worried that these brave people might misinterpret my visit to Hungary. They need have no fear. I have no illusions about Communism and its methods.'

Later in the spring of 1984 George Soros, the multi-million-aire Hungarian-American, called on us in Roger's flat. Soros had left Hungary as a 21-year-old in the 1950s. At the London School of Economics he had come under the influence of Karl Popper, whose great book *The Open Society and Its Enemies* shaped Soros's thinking – as it did the thinking of two generations of post-war students – from the moment he read it. As his Quantum Fund made repeated coups on global stock markets, Soros gained a legendary reputation as an investor. My preconceived idea of a brash tycoon was instantly undone by his wide friendly face, and intense, rather feline manner. There were still echoes of his origins in the intonation of his quiet speaking voice. He asked pertinent questions, to which he expected equally pertinent answers; though having received a reply he rarely made any immediate observation. He had the habit, with perhaps something of affectation in it, of coming to very rapid decisions.

Soros told us of the Open Society Institute he was forming in Budapest, the city of his childhood, for studies in economics, management and the humanities. Hungary was his priority, but he was prepared to help us in Czechoslovakia on certain precise conditions. He would not commit to stipends, but would support individual projects that reflected Popper's ideals. As a start he would give us 10,000 dollars to finance the production of a Czech language digest of political thought, with three Western editors who would take respective responsibility for conservative, centrist and socialist contributions. It was a project that we had long hoped to undertake. On telephoning his office the following day, we learnt that the money had already been transferred into our bank account.

The Sainsbury Foundation and the Esmé Fairbairn Trust had also offered financial help, but we had to think of more ways of raising money – and it might as well be fun. When the idea of a concert fell through, we settled on making use of my house in the Cotswolds to hold a fête. I promised half the proceeds to Quenington Church, just across the stream from the front lawn. The rest would go towards the Czech dissidents.

The morning of the fête was one of those radiant early summer days when the warm sun filters through a still haze of light. We pinned posters on boards and trees in all the surrounding villages and asked Bamber Gascoigne, who had become a national figure through his hosting of the TV quiz show 'University Challenge', to open the event. He had his heart in the cause and in front of a large gathering made an impassioned plea for Czechoslovakia. Then, turbaned, bejewelled and swathed in silk, Diana Phipps as 'Madame Polasky' took up position in a wooden hut, its walls stapled with maroon-coloured cotton, and began soothsaying behind a cloudy crystal ball. Within minutes a line of customers formed in the orchard outside her door, stretching finally – as her sessions lengthened – some thirty yards through the trees and long grass out onto the gravel path beyond.

By and by there was a hitch, albeit one which was to double our takings. I had originally asked the American novelist Alison Lurie, an expert fortune-teller with tarot cards, to play Madame Polasky. Because her train was very late she arrived long after Diana's triumphant beginning and was quite put out when her understudy seemed disinclined to surrender her position. Striding to the front of the queue, she more or less ordered Diana out of the hut. But Diana was now in demand and revelling in her new-found powers. So, while Alison occupied the hut, Diana swept up her cushions and installed herself a few yards away in the cow parsley, where she continued to attract troops of customers under the elongated branches of two weeping pears.

Halfway through the fête, a rather startling busload of Jamaicans appeared from London, brought down by Roy Kerridge, a *Spectator* essayist with whom for several months past I had been going on Sunday evenings to God of Prophecy services in Kensal Rise. Roy and I were usually the only white people in the church, in which the priest's missionary exhortations would be answered by compulsive hallelujahs and hypnotic spiritual chants from a packed congregation. Several times, at Roy's request, they had prayed for Charlie.

So these were some fifty of our church friends, arrived in Gloucestershire in the cause of 'Bibles behind the Iron Curtain'. Women, children and men shining with goodness poured out of the bus, thronging our wild garden. I have a photograph of a group of Jamaican children at Roger's target stall, for all the world like a squad of child guerrillas in the jungle. The grownups stationed themselves beside the river, belting out hymns above the sound of water gushing from the mill race. Indoors, against a backdrop of old books and heavy oak furniture, Roy's black half-sister, Zenga Longmore, in turquoise trousers and attended by her perfumed poodle, sang unaccompanied pre-war songs, quite unfazed by the chatter of people strolling in and out.

To our annoyance, word of Soros's support had leaked out, prompting an approach by the Czech exile Jan Kavan to share contacts and give him funding. 'You owe it me,' was his line. 'I've kept things going on a shoestring for years.' The claim of this controversial and complicated character that we owed him a favour harked back to an earlier encounter. Having fled to England after the Soviet invasion in 1968, he had for years been supplying the West with *samizdat* and Charter 77 material, much of it printed by his Palach Press in a cramped little flat in Soho. He had developed a sophisticated courier service, having fitted a concealed compartment into a Volkswagen van, in which books and light equipment could be smuggled across the Czech border. In 1981, two years before I became a trustee, he had requested a large sum from the Jan Hus to act as its regular conduit, being even then under the impression that the Foundation was brimming with endowments.

While the trustees were doing their homework and trying to make up their minds whether Kavan was trustworthy, there was a calamity. Following a tip-off, the Volkswagen was stopped and dismantled at the frontier with Austria. Materials were discovered, not only from his own operation but from three or four other émigré organisations that were using his service. Arrests followed. Seventeen dissidents were accused of conspiring with a foreign power to subvert the Republic, seven of them being detained in prison without trial for over a year. The last straw was a Thames TV feature, *The Last Round-Up?*, in which it was claimed that the police had found a comprehensive list of underground contacts in the van. In the circumstances it could hardly have come at a surprise to Kavan when the trustees decided not to pursue his proposition. Nevertheless, the refusal had rankled.

Kavan's renewed approach made the trustees even more wary. Personally, although I rather enjoyed his surliness, if only as a challenge, I found his secretive manner disconcerting. 'I have many contacts,' he told me, 'far more than yours.' No doubt this was true, but in that case why was he so interested in ours? He was also somewhat ostentatiously socialist, which I knew would raise the suspicions of Bratinka and Alena Hromádková back in Prague. After much debate we eventually arranged for Paul Flather, whose political sympathies would certainly be less offensive to him than mine or Roger's, to attend Palach Press's trustees meetings. Paul was, however, to make it clear that there would be no two-way flow of information.

Many years later Kavan was accused of collaborating with the secret police, an accusation of which he was not finally acquitted until 1996. Our flirtation with him caused dreadful anxiety to our dissident friends, who had been brought up in an atmosphere of constant betrayal and had no confidence in their compatriots abroad. Kavan's parents both had much to answer for. His father, Pavel, had been a zealous Stalinist until an internecine Party struggle in 1952 led to his conviction on trumped-up charges in the notorious Slansky show trial. His mother, Rosemary, an Englishwoman, was warm and well-liked, but she, too, was an ideological extremist. In her book *Freedom at a Price* she exhibited no remorse at all for their complicity in the reign of terror.

So far as I know, Jan Kavan never let us down. We took great precautions to keep him well away from any of our secrets.

And perhaps he had rebelled against his parents' beliefs. Nevertheless, in retrospect I look back with real regret at our having raised the unnecessary fear of infiltration among our contacts in Prague and Brno. God knows, they had enough to fear without our adding to their burdens.

Roger always said of Kavan[1] that he looked and behaved too much like a secret agent to be one. Moreover, he added later, you should always remember the difference between him and most of his political accusers – that he did something for his country, while they did nothing. I am inclined to think that we should accept that verdict and let the matter rest.

Later in the summer of 1984 I accepted an invitation, along with Roger Scruton and Caroline Cox, to give a paper to a summer conference at Bradford University on the theme of 'Peace Teaching in Higher Education'. The speaker before me was a reader in Peace Studies at the Open University. Peace Education, his synopsis explained, was a 'consciousness-raising process, based on general theory, prescriptions and strategies for change'. It involved 'mutual development of reasoning skills, positive (caring) goals and positive (caring) actions, emancipated from the damaging ideologies associated with cultural and social location and the concept of legitimacy'. He finished his lecture to a rapturous ovation from a packed auditorium.

On my way to the conference hall I had passed bookstalls stacked with anti-American essays. The banknotes at the checkout counter were stamped with the CND logo. The three of us had obviously been cast in the role of warmongers, to give balance to the proceedings. Nervously conscious that this would be my first ever public speech, I quoted Havel on the ambiguity of peace in a totalitarian society and argued that the disarmament lobby itself was the chief menace to international security.

I was interrupted by the contemptuous guffaws of a man

---

1 Kavan is now Deputy Prime Minister of the Czech Republic. In April 2000 he was put in charge of the Secret Service with responsibility for Foreign Intelligence. The following month a Czech publisher brought out his secret police files (1969–71) which topped the bestseller list.

with a thin pointed beard and the theatrical sobbing of two young women at the back. A Professor Fahey rose to say that he had not travelled all the way from the USA to hear the East-West conflict discussed in such reactionary terms. Having travelled from Australia, Professor Mack declared himself entitled to be even angrier. Foot-stamping and shouting broke out and grew to a crescendo. As the moderator lost control, the platform speakers decided to call it a day and repaired to the bar, leaving the hall in a state of pandemonium. It was a relief to find Caroline and Roger there, offering me a drink and moral support.

Next morning it occurred to me that my more left-leaning fellow trustees might be as much shocked to read of my contribution to the fiasco as I was shocked at the inclusion of CND courses in the primary and secondary school curriculum. Once, after one of my regular lunches with Alan Montefiore at Balliol, I had drawn his attention to a *Times* leader written by Charlie the previous evening. I had thought it particularly cogent on the disarmament issue. Alan dutifully read it, gave me a pitying shake of the head and said no more. Over coffee, I tried Bill Newton-Smith. 'Utter crap, if you don't mind my saying so.' As I have remarked before, it was an exceptionally divided era in British political thinking.

I wrote up the conference for *Encounter,* sending the article to Alena in Prague and Marcin Król in Warsaw. By underground channels, of course – an irony that would have been lost on the peace-loving audience at Bradford.

If we thought Charlie's cancer was a secret, we were wrong. I learnt much later that Rupert Murdoch knew the whole story from the outset. Charlie had decided that it was his duty to confide in Duke Hussey, the chief executive of the holding company, Times Newspapers, but had urged him to tell nobody else. Reluctant to hide a matter of such importance from his proprietor, Hussey had gone straight to Murdoch. He told him Charlie could live 'for anything from three months to five years'. (Hussey was, incidentally, also chairman of the Royal Marsden cancer hospital.) Murdoch instructed Hussey to take care of Charlie's medical and nursing bills and any equipment he needed, making it clear that he would remain editor until the day he died, so long as his mind was not affected. With that Murdoch closed the subject and never spoke of it to Hussey again.

Charlie's life revolved now entirely round the office. As he grew more immobile he would arrive in Gray's Inn Road at ten in the morning and stay there all day, returning home to bed by eleven after a working dinner. When he was forced to spend time in the Royal Free Hospital, the paper would set up a bed-side office for him, with a conference telephone system. The more his care became dependent on professional nursing, the more acutely aware I was of our powerlessness to help him. Spontaneous physical expressions of affection were made impossible by the pain of being touched and the fragility of his bones. Tara and Luke could never hug their father. They could not even play nearby, in case they inadvertently jogged him. Fortunately Luke, having reached the age of thirteen, wanted to follow his brother to boarding school; and with both sons away during the term neither of them would witness their father's worst moments of agony. I gave up theatre design, pre-ferring to paint in my studio at home, but continuing to make short trips behind the Iron Curtain. Irrational as it may sound, I felt somehow that by contributing in my small way to the alle-viation of Eastern Europe's vast collective tragedy, I could by a sort of proxy also do something to assuage Charlie's pain.

The summer ended with a sense of foreboding. There was dramatic news from Poland. In late July, in a ruse to soften the West into lifting sanctions, General Jaruselski ordered an amnesty to celebrate the fortieth anniversary of Polish Social-ism, freeing a few hundred Solidarity leaders and tens of thou-sands of common criminals. Straight after their release most of the Solidarity leaders went to St Kosta for Popiełuszko's Service of Thanksgiving. As they walked towards the church the con-gregation turned into a large crowd. Within minutes the crowd became a demonstration. At the church entrance Popiełuszko and Michnik appeared together framed in the doorway, Michnik giving the victory sign. There were roars and cheers for the rebirth of Solidarity. To the anonymous watchers in the shadows it was clear that Popiełuszko would have to be liquidated.

Dramas of a different kind were also brewing in Prague. Roger Scruton reported that Alena Hromádková was being followed everywhere by the political police and subjected to intimidation, questioning and harassment at work. Many years later, when we gained access to the secret police files, we learnt that the opening of the dossier on Roger dated to this period, based on his contact with Alena. An exile called Paul Moritz was deputed by the Czech Embassy to lurk around his flat in Bayswater – an unrewarding task, as Roger was usually out of town.

Alena, with her resolute and defiant character, had managed to keep her spirits up, but the authorities were determined to discover as much as they could about her activities and to develop incriminating evidence against her. I was anxious for her, particularly when I learned that Karel Palek's coded letter warning us not to send her any visitors had failed to reach us. When one of our student couriers turned up at Alena's apartment she was still at work; her mother, who opened the door, feigned total ignorance and the student was cool-headed enough to follow our emergency procedure and leave immediately with an apology for calling at the wrong address – fortunately unobserved by the police.

Hejdánek was less overtly threatened than Alena, but only because the authorities believed they already knew all they needed to know about him. His back was causing him serious trouble and he received his visitors in hospital. Some of us suspected that after so many years of stress there might be a psychological element to his condition, but the pain was real enough. Petr Rezek had temporarily taken over his seminars, using Hejdánek's apartment, which was raided as regularly as ever. There was pressure on foreigners, too. A Dutchman on his way to a seminar was intercepted at Prague airport and turned back.

Despite these escalating tensions I saw no real reason to postpone my next visit to Czechoslovakia. It would be almost a year to the day since my first.

Eight

For some days before each journey behind the Iron Curtain I used to have sleepless nights, seized in the early hours with fear of arrest. So far as I know, I first appear in the Czech secret police files in 1985, a year after Roger, but there can be no certainty, since hundreds of archives went missing in the weeks before the fall of Communism. The records that remain suggest that the police thought at first that we were working individually, with what they called the 'illegal Church': it was not until 1986 that they identified the Jan Hus as a subversive organisation.

Whether I was a marked woman or not, the glazed preoccupied manner I had cultivated to disguise my agitation worked again at the border and I entered without being stopped. Once out into the centre of Prague, travelling in the trams and walking the dingy streets, I shed my fear, elated and liberated as always by this fascinating city asleep in its beautiful past. I was looking forward immensely to seeing Alena, Petr Rezek and the others – and above all Bratinka.

My first port of call was the Obecní Dům. Some of the most intense hours of my life have been snatched behind the heavy glass doors of this café-restaurant. Warmed by a blast of foetid air, I sank into a scarred plush red leather bench against the window. If you had a fondness for decayed turn-of-the-century architecture and seedy, sullen waiters in stained black uniforms, and if you didn't mind cockroaches or the smell of sweat, beer, smoke and decayed food, then here was the place to be, in this majestic building, which housed on its first floor a magnificent concert hall and possessed one of the few great untouched Art Nouveau interiors in Europe. In the centre of

[67]

the room stood an Art Nouveau aquarium, and against the wall an Art Nouveau cigarette machine. Even the lifts dated back to the beginning of the 1890s.

Coffee, if you could place an order, was served on the ground floor, where thirty or so marbletop tables with upright wooden chairs scarcely filled the huge space. While I waited, I stared at the old wall mosaics by the light of the wide windows with their mauve-brown tattered curtains and struggled to read Czech newspapers on wooden sticks. The coffee, when it came, was grainy, with the consistency of treacle. Sitting here in what seemed another century, I was able to blot out for a moment images of Charlie's pain. Within the hour, my courage now fully revived, I was out in the streets again.

I had first to deposit my luggage. This time, on the introduction of a mutual friend, I was staying with Daniel Spička, a Czech architect with a roué charm, and his English wife, Victoria. They lived with their two daughters and Daniel's aged father in a large 1930s house in a suburb in the north-west district of Prague that had once been the village of Smíchov. Roger, who knew the Czech scene better than any of us, disapproved. The Spičkas were not connected to the Czech opposition and Daniel might even be under pressure to report on me. There was also the point that I might be compromising my hosts. I waved the problem aside – they would have no idea where I was going during the day. But Roger's caution was justified. Daniel later admitted that he had gone through my waste-paper basket, where he found coded instructions on scraps of paper.

Daniel's passion for early music and late nights often took him to the centre of Prague, where he played in a baroque ensemble, seldom returning home before midnight. I was therefore much thrown together with Victoria, whose straightforwardness was a haven from Prague's ubiquitous intrigue. She willingly played the part of guide. One afternoon we crept up a flight of stairs together into the Great Hall of the university library to see its dark murals, its tapestry of Charles IV and its ancient astronomical globes on pedestals among the blackened old oak bookshelves. Another day she took me to St James's Church, hidden away in a maze of small streets, to show me the stucco relief above the entrance doors depicting biblical characters stretching their arms towards Heaven. Whatever time Victoria could spare from the grinding search for basic household goods for her family, she spent on learning the city's secret charms.

Petr Rezek lived close by the Spičkas. I had no difficulty in locating the apartment again, but I was alarmed at my conspicuousness. The block was under renovation and there were workmen everywhere, many of them chattering down at me from the scaffolding like birds in a tree. I found Rezek in, writing at his desk in bright sunlight, wearing a peaceful expression and surrounded by his engravings. He preferred to talk outside and offered to walk me to my next destination, the Kučeras. On the way he launched into the latest chapter of his personal life, in such a sunny a frame of mind that I temporarily forgot about his mercurial moods. His mistress, for whom he was in the process of divorcing his wife, no longer wanted to live with him, leaving him with a second flat on his hands, acquired in exchange for stoking the boilers for a large apartment block in Rubešova Street. He had been depressed for a while about his mistress's change of heart, but he was beginning to see advantages in having two flats. Rubešova Street was a prime site in the heart of Prague, far superior to the location of Karel Palek's and Pavel Bratinka's boiler houses.

As we talked about his planning for the academic term ahead, Rezek grew aggressive and demanding. Irritated by his attitude, I said that we also had a bone to pick with him. We were angry about Karel Hubka, who worked at the Academy of Sciences and had been introduced to us as a friend and former pupil of Rezek. He had completed a two-year underground philosophy course the previous autumn and according to Rezek was one of his best students. Obsessed by analytical philosophy, Hubka had badgered us for an invitation to Britain. With great difficulty, Kathy Wilkes had arranged for him to spend three weeks at the Institute of Classical Studies in London and he had finally been granted a visa.

'Hubka's not coming back,' I said. 'Why on earth didn't you let us know he was the sort of person who might defect?' Two days after Hubka's arrival he had told us that, with the tacit compliance of his wife and daughter, he meant to make his future teaching philosophy in Britain. His wife and daughter would understand. It was quite outside the Trust's remit to sub- sidise a defector. One by one we had explained to Hubka – some- times for hours on end – that university employment would be virtually impossible for him to come by, but he had flatly refused to contemplate any form of non-academic work. This was the first and last defection we had to cope with and was all the more frustrating because he had no sense of the refugee's obligation to his adopted country to work his passage the hard way. Moreover, the word from Czechoslovakia was that his family had known nothing of his plans and were devastated.

Rezek shrugged his shoulders. 'It's nothing to do with me. You should solve your own problems,' he said, walking on ill- humouredly.

The street was no place for a row and I tried to brighten the atmosphere. I had news that I thought would please him. At the last trustees' meeting we had agreed to establish a monthly courier service rather than continue risking coded postcards, which often did not arrive. The new system would be more effective, but it required Rezek to be at home on the first Satur- day of every month or, if no one came, the third Wednesday. Far from being mollified, he pointedly ignored what I had told him and returned to his demands. He wanted more Plotinus and Virgil, as well as a long list of recordings – four versions, for comparative purposes, of each of *Carmen* and *Don Gio- vanni,* together with most of the works of Wagner, plus a video and a Walkman. He was the only dissident I met who was not embarrassed to ask for things for himself. I was taken aback by the scale of his requests, although once my annoyance had subsided I have to admit I found his enthusiasm for opera so persuasive that I always supported his cause at trustees' meetings.

We paused to enter a rickety doorway off the street. It led to a rough one-room café with two tables made of cheap formica. Rezek ordered two glasses of a strange white spirit and I slipped between the pages of a book the £180 due to him. Then, having finished our drinks, we went on down the steep hill, arriving as close to the Kučeras as Rezek dared go. Before saying goodbye, he offered to get the bus ticket for my journey to Brno next day. From that moment, until the end of my stay, I was passed carefully by hand, like a parcel of *samizdat*, from one dissident to another.

From the Kučeras I went to Alena's. Soon Bratinka arrived to drive me away in his grey Trabant. As we bounced up and down along the cobbled streets, Bratinka likened the skimpy plastic-like car to a sewing machine. He wanted to introduce me to two of his closest colleagues, Václav Benda and Václav Havel.

The meeting was to be in Benda's flat. All I knew of our host was that he was held in exceptionally high regard as a leading light in the Charter movement and as the founder of the Committee for the Unjustly Persecuted.

We were ushered into the hallway by his teenage daughter. Peering down the passage I saw ahead of us an exceedingly fat, long-haired figure who appeared to be more or less nude and encircled by women, like a pasha being anointed by his harem. As I came closer, I saw that he was having his hair cut, wearing bathing trunks and a skin-coloured T shirt.

The large flat where we now found ourselves was the equivalent of a dissidents' salon. Bratinka was used to Benda's eccentricities – Ralph Walker once noted that he 'found it disconcerting that he changed his trousers in the middle of the conversation' – and the two men had a casual exchange of words before I was introduced. Somewhat put out by Benda's appearance, I was stuck for words and was not in the mood to start a conversation. Not that I would necessarily have learned much if

I had. Denis Keefe, second secretary at the British Embassy in Prague, told me that at his own first meeting with Benda, Bratinka had also been the interpreter. Unknown to the others, Keefe had a smattering of Czech and was astonished to find that Bratinka was editing Benda's words as much as translating them. Moreover, Keefe was often left out of the conversation while the two argued vigorously, with Bratinka refusing point blank to translate some of Benda's replies. Evidently he could not bear to have Keefe take away the wrong impression of Czech dissident thinking.

Bratinka led me into the sitting room, where two other Charter spokesmen were in conversation by the window. The subject of their discussion was the rise of the previously unknown Mikhail Gorbachev. Bratinka's assiduous weekly reading of journals in the American Embassy made him one of the most respected Soviet-watchers. He told us that since Stalin's death Gorbachev had been working his way up in provincial political departments in the south. Before the assassination of Stalin's secret police chief, Beria, he had been in Moscow, where he had been active in the Communist youth movement. He owed his surprise appearance in the Politburo to another head of the KGB, Yuri Andropov. Despite these sinister beginnings, Gorbachev was being portrayed as a reformist. Bratinka's interpretation of the sequence of events was that Gorbachev was a Party *apparatchik* who had gained the trust of the KGB and was now being groomed for the leadership.

Bratinka agreed with Mrs Thatcher's assessment of Chernenko's health – he would not last long. On the frequent occasions when he was too ill to appear at the Politburo's weekly meetings, it was Gorbachev who took the chair. Moreover, during the summer Gorbachev had led a Soviet delegation to the funeral of the Italian Party leader Enrico Berlinguer. The Italians, with their soft brand of Euro Communism, had been the only party in Western Europe to have condemned the Soviet invasion of Czechoslovakia. Since then, their relations with the USSR had been icy. Clearly a thaw was on the way. 'This can have but one meaning,' Bratinka explained in his carefully con-structed English. 'It portends a change which goes beyond mere tactics, for it is grounded in the Soviet Union's financial bank-ruptcy, and its realisation that the technological race is lost. When Mikhail Sergeievich ascends the throne, those who place him there will pin on his shoulders the cloak of peacemaker.'

With that, he turned up the volume of the BBC World Ser-vice, which had all the while been purring in the background. The broadcast for which they had been waiting contained a Charter 77 statement about the Nobel Prize, recently won by the dissident poet Jaroslav Seifert, whom the Czech authorities had falsely claimed as their own. Benda never joined us. My last glimpse of him as we headed off to Havel was of a wispy dome being massaged in a room off the passage.

As an admirer of his plays and essays I was curious to meet Havel. It was normally the policy of the Jan Hus to steer clear of dissidents who were already in the sights of the Western media; others needed us more. But I knew it would be easier for me to fight his cause if I knew him personally. Besides, he was a friend of Bratinka. He had only recently been released from a five-year prison sentence, during which he had written his famous *Letters to Olga*. Since he had no intention of remain-ing silent it was on the cards that the authorities would put him back behind bars before long.

Havel's flat was on the attic floor of a building with a sweep-ing view over the River Vltava. The walls and the stairwell out-side were covered with abstract paintings, many of them by his brother Ivan. We were let in by his wife Olga, a stalwart woman, her beauty worn down by exhaustion and strain. We found him in the sitting room reclining on a modern sofa with pale cushions, smaller and more delicately featured than he appeared in his photographs. He was, as usual, smoking.

With Bratinka there to translate, the conversation was relaxed, despite Havel's reserved manner. After a while we started to look at some photographs that Bratinka had brought with him. For years the two of them had spent fortnightly weekends together in Havel's country cottage in Hradeček, north of Prague, where they talked philosophy and literature with friends. Sometimes there would be as many as ten to fifteen participating in what was effectively a cross between a masterclass and a workshop. Across the road from the cottage the police had erected a watchtower on stilts. Bratinka had some good photographs of the scene. They laughed as they recalled the relays of observers and speculated on the reaction of the Ministry of the Interior as it struggled with interminable tapes of learned academic discourse.

Before leaving, I asked Havel whether there was anything I could do for him in London, perhaps in connection with the theatre. He thought not, and I started to make my goodbyes. Then he had an afterthought. Bratinka had told him I could sometimes help with the press. He had recently written, but had been unable to deliver, a speech, of which a shortened version had appeared in Paris. Could I perhaps get it published in full in English? I promised to do my best.

It was nearly 9 pm. Bratinka had to get back to his family in the Leninova district and I was to collect my ticket to Brno from Rezek. Bratinka dropped me nearer my destination than he should have – only two blocks short of Rubešova Street – but even so I found the entrance hard to locate. It would have been more convenient to have met at Rezek's other place near the Spičkas, but he had insisted on making the rendezvous at his second home.

He must have heard my boots clatter up the stone steps to the first floor, for the door swept open before I had time to knock. He looked nervy. Over his shoulder, I could just pick out a square room empty of furniture with a huge double mattress on the floor. Handing me my ticket, he made it obvious that he did not want me to go. In the dim light, I saw with apprehension the expression on his face turn to an all-too-familiar glower. A brief struggle ensued. Stuffing the ticket in my pocket, I ran down the stairs and made my way on foot across the town and up the steep hill to the Spičkas. There I met another hazard. My key would not turn in the lock and the house was in darkness. Everyone was in bed except Daniel, who had not yet returned from another of his late nights. I threw pebbles up at their bedroom window, causing Victoria some alarm, but she finally opened the door and heard my story sympathetically. Next morning, as I came down the stairs, I overheard her joking to Daniel about my previous night's encounter. Far from being amused, Daniel was indignant. I had slighted the honour of Czech manhood by rejecting Petr Rezek's advances. 'She may be attractive *now*,' I heard him say, 'but that won't last for ever.'

I was mildly surprised to hear myself being talked about in this way. I had become so used to idolising my friends for their heroic dissidence that I had fallen out of the habit of thinking of them as ordinary human beings.

Nine

Three hundred kilometres south of Prague – in the heart of Moravia – the concrete station where the bus ejected its passengers gave a grim foretaste of Brno. The city's days as a great artistic centre were long gone. Most of the medieval quarter had been pulled down to make way for nineteenth-century industry. Nevertheless, bits and pieces of ancient history remained. At the foot of Špilberk Castle, a prison fortress of the Hapsburgs, lay a cobbled market place and the older original prison, now part of the Town Hall. A hint of pre-First World War opulence still clung to a row of houses and shops reminiscent of Vienna. I was able, too, to pick out a few buildings from the Brno school of functionalist architecture. It was here that the leading light of this particularly Central European style, Mies van der Rohe, designed and built his first house, the Tugendhat Villa, which lay abandoned amid thistles and ragwort on the edge of town. It was fashionable to admire the villa; personally, I thought it almost as hideous as Communist architecture.

Jiří Müller lived in the suburbs. I was to make contact with him to put the finishing touch to a programme of seminars, over which Alena had acted as intermediary. I could not risk a taxi even half way to his house – Brno had recently won the Warsaw Pact award for the best policed city in the Soviet bloc. Bugging equipment had been installed in restaurants, theatres, galleries, shops, private homes and cars; even, word had it, in the streets. Trudging on foot with my bags, I followed with difficulty the map Alena had sketched out for me until I found 23 Chudobova Street, a simple two-storey house with a small front garden. I was welcomed by a pale, strong young man. His honest grey eyes looked straight into mine. It was easy to believe that this was the master mind of the Moravian underground. He must have been in his forties, but prison darkness is notorious for keeping its inmates' skin young. He swept me into his hallway with a beaming smile.

His story was familiar. As a student at Charles University he had been arrested and imprisoned for 'subversion'. His crime was to have mobilised opposition to the Soviet occupation and to have distributed leaflets at election time informing people of their right to abstain. He spent the next five years confined with two others in a tiny cell (this treatment was reserved for political prisoners: convicted thieves, rapists and murderers were allowed to roam freely about the compound). Shortly after his release, Jiří signed Charter 77, founded a *samizdat* publishing house and made contact with Western sympathisers. Betrayed by the capture of Kavan's courier service, he was jailed again for subversion, charged now with 'collaboration with foreign powers'. As a result of international pressure, however, he was released almost immediately.

On gaining freedom, he changed tactics. Henceforth he would operate in the 'grey world' – the disillusioned who fell short of outright dissidence and were able to remain in legitimate employment. He cultivated and put in touch with each other a vast network of disaffected students, artists, teachers and officials, carefully avoiding the creation of an underground ghetto that would invite police harassment. In view of his previous record, he had to conceal his own role and work through others who were not suspected by the authorities. Few of those he brought together ever met him face to face, and apart from his wife Broňa only two others understood the full extent of his ambition, which was no less than the undermining of the Party's monopoly on information and communication.

We sat round a small wooden table near the window of his sitting room, communicating in silence with paper and pencil, Broňa translating twice over. What Jiří wanted from us, she wrote, was not philosophy lectures but talks on Western life, preferably with a social and ethical dimension. What exactly, for example, were the aims of feminism? What were the dynamics of the Green Movement? Jiří would not appear at the talks, Broňa wrote. The host would be Petr Oslzlý of the avant-garde Theatre on a String, Brno's best known stage director. There were seven theatres in the town, but Oslzlý's alone was packed every night, its audiences drawn by the excitement – and the coded messages – of his productions.

It was of the utmost importance, Broňa said, to protect the secrecy of Jiří's link with Oslzlý, who was not compromised. When I left the Müllers, we went through a series of elaborate evasive manoeuvres. With Jiří at the wheel of his little two-doored Trabant, we sped off towards the centre of the town. After a few hundred yards he stopped abruptly, backed down a street and waited. Three times in three different streets we repeated this exercise, with Jiří's eyes glued to the mirror to see if we were being followed. Then we travelled two miles out of Brno and waited again. Finally I was transferred into another car. Jiří would not see me any more on this visit, but wished me luck and sent warm regards to Roger Scruton as he slammed the door and watched me depart with a bearded stranger to my next rendezvous.

Petr Oslzlý was blond and thick-bearded, with an eirenic aura, enhanced by his golden-haired wife, Eva, and his two young daughters, who swam in their parents' wake like Rhine-maidens. His apartment was light and airy. His girls had perfect manners, with not a hint of unruly behaviour – a quality I had often noticed in the children of dissidents. As for Eva, it was her strength of character and the stability of her marriage to Petr that had tipped the scales in Jiří Müller's decision to take the Oslzlýs into his confidence. That Petr Oslzlý should have existed at all amid the deadening drabness of Brno was a triumph of the human spirit. His English was rough, my Czech and German stumbling at best, but his alchemy cut easily through these inconveniences to uncover wide avenues of common ground in poetry and music, in literature, history and painting. Everything about his character was original, open and from the heart. There was no question of disguising our conversation with notes or hushed voices. With the help of several glasses of slivovitz I was wrapped in Oslzlý's formative years in experimental theatre under the Polish director Jerzy Grotowski, wrapped in his passion for the films of Eisenstein, particularly the Odessa Steps sequence in *The Battleship Potemkin*. He argued late into the night in true central European style, leaving me to totter to bed with my mind in a turmoil. He had the energy of an impresario and the teacher's gift, met with only once or twice in a lifetime, of being able to take an idea or a work that you previously thought you knew and turn it through the whole spectrum of colours so that you saw it in a constantly fresh light. I secretly wished I could design one of his productions.

The short trips abroad which Oslzlý was permitted to make with his theatre had led to friendships which provided the camouflage for his underground activities. A few days before each talk he would pass the word round that he would be 'at home' for a small party. As a precaution against infiltrators and possible police questioning, no guest would be told more than that. There was more at risk for Oslzlý than for Jiří Müller, who had already lost his career. In the event that the house was raided any visitor from the West would be passed off as a theatrical contact who had looked in and was staying the night. Translation would be supplied by Mikin Pospíšil, who was partly, but not fully, in the secret. Pospíšil had been sacked from Brno University for refusing to join the Party and was now in a dead-end job teaching English at the State language school.

Oslzlý took note of my list of new visitors lined up for the next three months, including Roger, who would be returning soon. I agreed also to give a talk on painting. Before I left, he took me to a doctor's house, where there was to be an outdoor party for artists. At the bottom of a garden that stretched up a steep hill covered with apple, pear and plum trees, we sat drinking beer in the gentle autumn afternoon. Wood fires gave out a delicious smell of burned sausages. Here Oslzlý introduced me to an artist he particularly admired, the sculptor Ján Šimek. Unable to communicate with me in English or German, Šimek cooked my meal in a saucepan above the flames before unwrapping his pieces of sculpture – forceful, magnetic figures in wood, coiled and contorted, as if poised to spring out with a mocking laugh.

Šimek kept his work at home, making room for it by gradually emptying his apartment of furniture. Neither he nor the others exhibiting in the doctor's garden could obtain the licence that would allow them access to public space. Their work had been rejected by a jury from the Union of Artists for failing to depict 'the heroism in the work and life of our workers, peasants and intelligentsia' or 'the graceful beauty of our native land'. Stylistically, however, there was a glimmer of hope. Socialist Realism was falling out of favour and the authorities were mouthing vague slogans about 'optimism', 'humanism' and a 'wide range of artistic possibilities'. Threatened for prosecution as a parasite, Šimek had so far survived. The previous month a policeman had visited him in his studio and ordered him to find work. 'Look,' Šimek had asked, turning from his carving, 'which of us here is "working" – you or I?'

After the barbecue, a painter with a long, thin, mournful face invited me to climb the hill with him. On either side of the path, sculptures and folders of etchings were laid out in the deep grass. To right and left, charcoal drawings on large sheets of paper were pinned to trees and rectangular oils on canvas stood propped against the tree trunks. At the top of the hill, out of earshot, the young man – almost a boy – plied me with questions about my own painting and the technique I used when working with acrylic paint, which dried so quickly. For this painter beside me there was nothing but despair. 'Tomorrow you will be in Vienna, no?' he said. 'I will never go to Vienna. I will never go to London. Can you imagine how it is to be free but in a prison? I can go to these places but then they will never let me return home. Some people, they can paint like this, like an animal in a cage. For me, it is too difficult to paint without happiness.' He stared out longingly towards Austria, twenty-five miles away to the south.

Ten

Only days after my return, a drama in Poland erupted. Father Popiełuszko had disappeared. He had been driven by a friend named Chrostowski to take a church service in Bydgoszcz, a small town four hours' drive from Warsaw. When he did not turn up for the early morning mass at St Kosta's next day there was immediate alarm. For eleven days the Polish people waited, hoping against hope. On 30 October – three weeks after he had been reported missing – his body was found in the Vistula, near Toruń: he had been thrown over a bridge, bound and gagged while still alive, weighted down by boulders.

On leaving Bydgoszcz, Chrostowski and Popiełuszko had been stopped by two secret policemen, who had forced them into a car. By some extraordinary feat Chrostowski had managed to open the door at speed and fling himself out. If he had not survived to tell the tale, the circumstances of Popiełuszko's death would have remained a mystery. With the nation close to anarchy, Jaruzelski blamed 'the antics of two low-level juniors in the Security Department' and set about trying to distance his Government from the murder. The assassins were duly apprehended and charged.

The way for us to tackle this disaster, we decided, was to treat the trial as the most important one to have taken place in Eastern Europe since the show trials of the '50s. We would record the proceedings with meticulous accuracy and give the maximum possible international publicity to the evidence and the verdict. That was the least we owed to Father Popiełuszko for his martyrdom.

The Polish legal system was a sorry amalgam of pre-war law and Communist insertions. What we needed was an independent observer of stature, with a good knowledge of Polish, to prepare a comprehensive transcript. Once we had recruited a suitable candidate in Dr Lammich, a German lawyer, we bought him a miniature tape-recorder, which I agreed to try and smuggle to Warsaw and deposit with an intermediary before the trial.

The problem was when could I go. At the beginning of January 1985, Rupert Murdoch and Charlie staged the first of many celebrations of the 200th anniversary of *The Times*, inviting 300 guests to the Festival Hall for a banquet and a concert with the Chicago Symphony Orchestra. More events were planned at regular intervals throughout the year. There was no way of excusing myself even if I had wanted to. There was, however, a brief opening in early February and I took my chance.

For once I was travelling without my usual heavy load of books and photocopier parts. But the tape-recorder was an incriminating object and had to be well hidden. Conveniently, I had filled my suitcase to bursting point with sumptuous theatrical dress material. For some time I had been corresponding with Małgorzata Król about our Early English opera project. She had wanted to mount a performance of a Gibbons and Locke work for a cast of twelve. This, however, was out of the question, so she had settled for the less ambitious *8 Songs for a Mad King* by Maxwell Davies. While I was trying to figure out the least expensive way to make King George's lavish costume, the dress designer Caroline Charles took me to her warehouse, where roll upon roll of embroidered satin, velvet and shot silk was stacked in trays against the walls, and invited me to take as much as I wanted 'for Poland'. It was the perfect gift for Małgorzata and the perfect concealment for the tape-recorder. (I was taking nothing for Marcin. In recent months he had become an 'official' dissident, sought after by the now more 'liberal' Government as testimony to its broadness of mind in permitting him and his journal to exist. He was quite comfortable in this peculiar position.)

Małgorzata was waiting at the airport barrier for me. She piled my luggage into her car and we went off to deposit the material with her seamstress. An hour later she dropped me with my precious load at a *samizdat* editor's office. Feeling much relieved to have completed my mission undetected, I travelled next day to Wrocław to see what I could do to help a theatre director who was under threat from the authorities. I stayed with the historian Dolek Juzwenko[1] (himself recently released from prison) and his doctor wife Krystyna in their tiny two-roomed apartment on the tenth floor of a concrete block of flats that was a labyrinth of evil-smelling passages and creaking lifts. Yet somehow they managed to live in style and grace. It was a fatal mistake to admire any of their lovely possessions – a book, a piece of china, a poster – for Krystyna would immediately press the object into my hand, saying 'Take it. Yes, take it! It's yours.'

Krystyna and I went for long walks together along the wide boulevards into the centre of Wrocław, where we sometimes shopped for supper. There was little to be seen on the shelves. Meat was still rationed; so was sugar. A consignment of oranges arrived but they were snatched up before we could reach them. Chocolate could only be sold to children. Outside in the street, old men and women appeared with baskets, selling meagre little collections of vegetables, everything exquisitely presented, fan-shaped or in tightly-knit rows. Living standards were as primitive as I had ever seen, far worse than in Czechoslovakia. 'Oh, this isn't Warsaw! Or Prague!' Krystyna said. But by the miserable standards of Wrocław, even provincial Brno was luxurious.

Another feature of street life was the frequent sight of nuns and priests. As we returned from shopping, a squat, stout little man emerged from a doorway, wearing a blue overcoat over his black cassock, and walked up the street in front of us. Many of the passers-by turned and stared or went to speak to him, or

---

1 Dolek Juzwenko is currently standing for the Polish senate. Krystyna is head of clinical pharmacology in Wrocław Medical School.

went down on their knees and crossed themselves as he passed. This was Father Ozhnohorski, a priest well known for his role in Solidarity.

Most of my meetings with the theatre director I had come to see were in the 'island', the oldest part of the city around the Cathedral with its ecclesiastical buildings. Here the Church's protective arm stretched around the alternative culture. I was taken into the crypt of a tiny Romanesque church, to a makeshift art gallery, Galeria na Ostrowie, to be shown an exhibition of banned artists, where a sculptor pressed on me a dozen or so of his tiny wooden carvings – small black-painted figurines and crucifixes. I rather disliked them but promised reluctantly to do my best to procure them a showing in England. The artist talked about a recent pilgrimage to Częstochowa: 13,000 people from Wrocław had walked there, and tens of thousands more from all over Poland. Dolek Juzwenko had given history lectures to the Wrocław pilgrims while they were on the march, using a megaphone.

I returned to the airport in good time for my departure. My ticket was checked without incident and I moved on to show my passport and visa at another kiosk. As I did so a grey-suited figure approached from my left and asked me to come with him. 'Why?' 'Because we wish to talk with you.' 'Why?' Without receiving a reply, I lamely agreed to be taken to the north wall of the airport, where a glass door slid back, revealing a room with a large window and a desk. Here I was introduced to a surly, thick-set, dark-uniformed woman of middle age who told me to come with her into a nearby cubicle where she intended to search me.

Alone with the woman in this tiny room I suddenly screamed. The more she tried to get at my bag, the more I lashed out, hitting her hard on the shoulder and arms. In spite of my notes being indecipherable, I was seized with an irrational fear that the scraps of paper wedged into the zipped inner pocket of my bag would endanger every one I had met. I threw myself into the corner and started tearing up my coded notes and addresses into minute pieces, at the same time continuing to kick and hit out. With strong, grabbing hands, the woman finally got what she wanted, but not before all my writing had been shredded – and bits of it swallowed – before her eyes. My collection of tiny black wooden crucifixes spilled out of their white envelope and stared up at me, stark and depressing.

After our first encounter, we both calmed down and the woman told me to remove my clothes. This was not a worry; I had nothing hidden. Nevertheless, it made me extremely angry, and I demanded to speak to Roger Boyes, of the *Times* office in Warsaw, with whom I had been staying as usual. After a long telephone conversation in Polish, Boyes was finally put on the line to me. Sounding more embarrassed than sympathetic, he told me that I was considered '*agresywna*' – aggressive. In my raw state, I wondered at his tone of voice. Why was he not offering me the words of encouragement I needed? But he was my only link with the outside world and I begged him to stay near the telephone.

Several years later Boyes confessed to me that he had been perplexed at the severity of my treatment, the strip-search, the sheer personal viciousness, especially since Jaruzelski's government was trying at the time to present a softer image and I had not visited 'dangerous' people in Solidarity's inner circle. His reaction when I called had been coloured by suspicion that I might have been up to something that might lead to the paper's Warsaw bureau being shut down. In a way he was right – though the danger had already passed.

My interview now came to an abrupt end. With a nod at my diary, notepad and books, which lay in piles on the table, my interrogators coldly announced that I could leave the country. They would be keeping everything except the unwanted wooden carvings. Back in the departure lounge, I found I had missed my plane by forty-five minutes. I was forced to buy a new ticket to London via Frankfurt. The only pleasure I had from my disagreeable experience was supplied by Tim Garton

Ash, who told me that his Polish wife had found it wonderfully cathartic to hear of my landing blows on her country's hated secret police.

Our friends in the underground secured Dr Lammich a place in the courtroom and slipped him the tape-recorder. Within a month of the trial's conclusion his 100-page report was in our hands. It was at the time the only authoritative account available in the free world and we gave copies to the Foreign Office, the State Department and a number of human rights organisations. We could not claim to have influenced the outcome of the trial, which ended in the conviction of the assassins while leaving unscathed the shadowy figures who had given them their orders. Nevertheless, we had some small consolation in that we had set a precedent for high-profile Western coverage of judicial proceedings behind the Iron Curtain. Just possibly the authorities might think twice the next time they contemplated silencing a dissident by murder.

In April I was telephoned by George Urban, a Hungarian exile, now head of Radio Free Europe, who had made his name through trenchant interviews of renegade Soviet sympathisers. He was a stalwart supporter of our cause and had recommended Roger Scruton and myself to the director of the newly formed NED (National Endowment for Democracy) in Washington. 'Make contact with Carl Gershman straight away. He's interested in backing you.' This promising piece of good fortune ran immediately into a hitch. The other trustees baulked at accepting American Government money. Was the NED a covert CIA operation? No, Gershman assured us when we met in Roger's flat, it was backed by both parties in Congress. It aimed to promote democracy in countries under totalitarian rule through educational grants. The boot was now on the other foot. Gershman needed proof that our work was valued by the right people in Czechoslovakia. We dispatched one of our messengers to Prague to smuggle out a letter from Václav Havel. He described the work of the Trust as 'very important to the sustaining of independent intellectual life, free political thought and cultural continuity in Czechoslovakia ... not only for the future of our country but in a more general sense: for the destiny and outlook of Europe are linked with the destiny and outlook of each European nation, and consequently with ours'. We forwarded Havel's letter to the NED and waited.

When the news came that we had been assigned a substantial grant for a long-term programme for the dissidents, far from being overjoyed Roger and I were afflicted with a sense of alarm. Being based in London, we would have to assume the lion's share of the work. What had once been an informal part-time activity threatened to turn into a full-time permanent commitment.

Chernenko was dead within a year of becoming leader and Gorbachev was already ushering in the changes foreseen by Bratinka. His early speeches, filled with slogans, called for *uskcorienie* (acceleration) and *democratznie* (democratisation). The West was supposed to glean messages of a partial conversion to capitalism and a reversion to *détente*. Later, when he spoke of *perestroika* (restructuring) and *glasnost* (openness), wishful thinkers interpreted *glasnost* as freedom of speech and *perestroika* as the dismantling of centralised planning and the introduction of market forces. How far the reforms were really supposed to go was, however, a matter of guesswork. Gorbachev's language was Delphic. On the ground, nothing seemed to have been thought through. As for guidance to the satellite countries, none was forthcoming. For the time being the leaders there were left completely in the dark.

The Czech Party, whose own brand of *glasnost* and *democratznie* had been crushed seventeen years earlier, was thrown into confusion by these developments. For outsiders it was even more impossible to predict what might happen. Roger and I agreed with the other trustees that we would go to Prague and Brno as soon as possible to sniff the air and set up new programmes.

The weekend before I was due to depart, Charlie collapsed

and became paralysed in his legs. We were expecting Robin Cook, the shadow Home Secretary, to look in for lunch with his wife on their way to the Badminton horse trials. Since there was no way of contacting them to warn them off, Charlie disguised the fact that he was unable to move by receiving Cook in his bedroom. After their departure, we summoned an ambulance, which took Charlie away to the Royal Marsden Hospital in Surrey. It was perhaps the bleakest moment of my life. That night he underwent a spinal operation, which temporarily relieved his agony but left him unable to stand. He would never be able to walk again.

I cancelled my planned Czech journey to stay with Charlie, by now probably alone in thinking there was still hope. His determination to live never wavered. His will had pulled him through each crisis and I still clung to the doctors' original prognosis that he could survive for up to ten years. Several miles from the centre of London, he continued to edit the paper, with relays of journalists visiting his bedside. Three weeks later he was back in the office, permanently confined to an electric wheelchair, a nurse constantly by his side.

By remaining in London, I was spared a second encounter with the secret police. In Brno Roger was arrested with Jiří and Broňa Müller. The visit had passed without disturbance until the second day, when the three of them drove to a park to begin a discussion in earnest. Having settled on a bench, his notebook on his knee, Roger glanced up to find two sinister young men looking down at him from what seemed to him for a split second a superhuman height. Then one, the taller and more dangerous-looking of the pair, said to him 'We know very well that you speak Czech, Mr Scruton. You will come with us for questioning, please.'

In the subsequent flicker of events, Roger's strongest impression was of the calm of the Müllers and the decisiveness with which they acted. Since Roger's passport was at their house, Jiří and Broňa were ordered to return in their own car, while the police followed with Roger. Jiří raced home, locking the door before the others arrived. Three minutes of banging brought him to the doorstep, but he refused either to fetch Roger's belongings or to allow the police to enter. It was for Professor Scruton, he said, to collect what was his. Finally the two policemen acquiesced, on condition that one of them acompany Roger everywhere. Fortunately his guard was easily embarrassed and Roger contrived enough time alone in the lavatory to destroy the incriminating pages of his notebook.

Taken to the police station, he underwent the classic interrogation method: the one questioner hard, menacing and insolent, the other apologetic, conciliatory, and seeming to offer avenues of escape. It soon transpired, however, that their instructions were to get rid of this subversive foreigner quickly and painlessly. He was accused of a non-existent offence and given three hours to leave the country.

On his return he reported ugly signs of trouble brewing in Prague for a music club called the Jazz Section. The Section was a furnace of youthful activity, a jazz concert organisation doubling as an unlicensed publishing house and a centre of popular culture. With 6,000 members, and growing by the day, its subversive potential was alarming the authorities. Its headquarters were repeatedly raided, its files ransacked and its manager, Karel Srp, removed from his official job in a state publishing house and put under round the clock surveillance. Srp's fate, like that of the club, hung in the balance.

Rather than delaying our reaction until the authorities had completed their dirty work, we plotted to forestall them. This was a project I could get on with at home, pushing friendly journalists to write about the Jazz Section and contacting Charles Alexander, the President of the International Jazz Federation, to solicit his support. We also got in touch with the Conservative MP Norman St John Stevas, who was due to make a speech in Budapest in the autumn under the auspices of the Helsinki Accord. If Czechoslovakia continued to persecute the Section, surely it could no longer be considered a signatory in good faith and should forfeit cultural ties with the West.

It was our standard practice to inform the Czech desk of the Foreign Office whenever one of our lecturers or trustees travelled to Prague, if only because we might need protection if something unpleasant happened. True, we had long given up hope of enlisting even a modicum of support for the cause of liberty. The officials noted that our visits were 'unhelpful'. We were 'unwise' to communicate with dissidents. Ministers were briefed that we were 'rocking the boat'. Now, however, under Mrs Thatcher, the climate looked brighter. East Europeans were being offered encouragement through increased economic and commercial links with Britain. More importantly, the Prime Minister was making Western aid conditional on internal political reforms. Human rights were back on the agenda. Perhaps after all we could try to interest the Foreign Office in the Jazz Section.

We had previously been in touch with Malcolm Rifkind, Minister of State for Eastern Europe, over the Hubka affair. When we had known for sure that Hubka could not be dissuaded from seeking asylum, Roger had written asking Rifkind to look on the case leniently. Rifkind had replied sympathetically. His Lithuanian Jewish background and his family's flight from Communism had given him the imagination to understand what we were trying to achieve in Czechoslovakia. During his recent visit to Warsaw – the first by a NATO minister since the introduction of martial law – he had shown that he was not overly concerned with Jaruzelski's sensitivities. He had made the unusual gesture of paying silent tribute at Father Popiełuszko's grave.

Roger and I now contacted Rifkind again and met with him for half an hour in his office. After taking him through a number of relatively minor requests we came to our main point. We had for some time been supplying the Foreign Office with detailed evidence of the persecution of Karel Srp – his officials could testify to that. We explained the Section's role in the lives of ordinary Czech people. Jazz had a special tradition in Czechoslovakia dating from the early years of the Republic, when jazz clubs sprang up all over Prague; its significance as an art form increased when it was outlawed during the Nazi occupation and again in the Stalinist era. Most of the Section's members were amateurs employed in normal occupations, perhaps belonging to a small band or practising the saxophone alone at home in the cellar. Might the Foreign Office support St John Stevas in highlighting harassment of the club as a violation of the Helsinki Accord? We could ensure the Section a high profile by arranging invitations for Czech jazz musicians and return visits from British groups, but without some official lifeline from the West we feared for the safety of Karel Srp.

Rifkind told us he would think things over. When his letter came, it revealed the limits to what he could offer, but its friendly tone was a source of real encouragement to all of us who were engaged in the campaign to save the Section.

With Roger now on the banned list, I was one of the few trustees who was still able to enter Czechoslovakia. Chuck Taylor, Kathy Wilkes and Bill Newton-Smith periodically applied for visas, only to be met with stony-faced refusal. But someone had to set up the programme for the start of the new academic year and it was up to me to do it. Charlie's condition appeared temporarily to have stabilised and I felt that it would not be letting him down to go. Even if I were arrested, it was unlikely I would be detained for long.

Nevertheless, I half hoped I would be denied entry. After my interrogation at Warsaw airport, it seemed likely that the Czechs would have a file on me. A message had come from the Juzwenkos in Wrocław to warn me that I had been followed continuously on my last visit (they knew this because Solidarity monitored the Polish secret police's short wave radios). Further, after the party the Juzwenkos had given for me at their home, one of the guests had been arrested. He was interrogated about me and asked what he thought he was doing visiting the home of a known trouble-maker and consorting with a British spy. We supposed that the Eastern European security forces pooled their information on suspicious visitors. (We were right but overestimated their efficiency. In June the Czech Ministry of the Interior had received a request from the Polish 'friends' for information about 'Jessica Douglas-Home, neé Gwynne, wife of the Editor of *The Times*'. The Czech police replied that they had none.)

My visa was slipped through the hatch at the Czech Embassy twenty-four hours before my scheduled departure. At the end of September, in more than ordinary trepidation, I was once more on a journey to Brno and Prague.

Eleven

Four months had passed since Roger's arrest and Jiří Müller, who had been lying low, felt able to meet me. Arriving at his house at 11.45, I sat down straightaway to a silent lunch of plums and suet dumplings sprinkled with poppy seed. As usual we denied ourselves talk until we were in a safe place. Jiří, his constitution hardened by practice, had fourteen dumplings. I took six. Presently I began to sense their effect, but I kept quiet as I was borne off at speed in Jiří's car, feeling like an extra in a gangster film. If we were followed, which from craning my neck to peer through the rear window I thought we were not, we certainly shook off our pursuers. We ended up in a hospital waiting room in the suburbs. It was an inspired choice of venue from the standpoint of security, and as my stomach got worse it occurred to me that the medical facilities might also come in useful. The hospital atmosphere, however, had horrible associations for me. I had a sudden desperate urge to know if Charlie was all right.

Jiří's newest project centred on Czechoslovakia's disastrous ecological situation. Relying on his extensive contacts in the 'grey zone' he was concocting a plan to identify informants in the Government departments through whom he could arrange 'information exchanges' with the West. This would entail elaborate subterfuge. The starting point would generally be a scientific article – heavily censored, of course – in a Czech journal. This would lead to an artless inquiry from Tom Burke, a freelance environmentalist in London, followed by an official visit to 'develop common problem-solving approaches'. Once they overcame their initial reticence, Jiří's sources unleashed a torrent of devastating data, which were analysed and documented by Burke. This method of working proved so successful that we were eventually able to duplicate it throughout the satellite countries, even in the USSR, collecting material right up to the fall of Communism.

Broňa and Jiří dropped me off near the Oslzlýs'. Although Broňa would come to one of my art lectures, they thought it best that neither of them should speak to me again on this trip. My first talk, on British portraiture from Hogarth to Bacon and Freud, was at seven in the evening.

I was presented as a stage designer friend on my way to Prague from Budapest. When I finished, there was disappointingly little discussion and Petr Oslzlý asked the students as they left why they had not been more responsive. One of them replied that they were not used to interaction – at their university course they just took notes. Letting me down as lightly as he could, Oslzlý added that this was a more diffident group than the self-confident literary set that he had invited to other events.

The truth that he was sparing me was that I had been rather boringly academic. Next time he wanted me to make my lecture more theatrical and to colour it with personal touches. This was untried territory for me. I slightly disapproved of artists who discussed their painting in public. Nevertheless, taking my dry script to bed I rewrote it from start to finish. The Czech painters I had met over the last two years often seemed stuck in 1960s abstraction, so I decided to give them a jolt.

I have always been a figurative artist [I began]. Abstract art does not interest me. Concerned with the beauty of patterns and shapes, it provides no tension, only watered down poetic feelings and undisciplined emotions. Figures say far more to me. Through their shape, colour and juxtaposition, I want to unlock valves of feeling which lead to a deeper sense of the reality of the image, and therefore return the onlooker to life more violently – to provide moments of recognition of what might be called the elemental truths about the figure and, through the figure, the human condition.

I like to start with the form clear and precise, to be as factual and as ordered as possible, but during the working of the paint to rely on accident and chance, to break away from the imposed structure. Risks must be taken in allowing the paint to find a life of its own. I try to keep the vitality of the accident. I do not know how the painting will turn out from the simple object that I set out to do; surprise takes over from intention quite early on; there is an inevitability about it; certain images get hold of you as you work; the canvas becomes a battleground for weeks, sometimes months, to come.

I was relieved to see that the apathetic audience of the previous evening was now alert, exchanging whispers and scribbling copious notes.

I begin by using large brushes which become smaller towards the completion of my canvas. I seldom place more than two or three images in a painting. The position of the body is all important. I put little detail into the face. My figures are often people I know. But I do not like having them in the room as I work. I keep to hand photographs I have taken. I prefer to be alone with the memory of the person, the memory of the deepest level of their personality, in painting to return them to themselves, working as close to the nervous system as I can.

Oslzlý came back to Prague with me to introduce me to Karel Srp. We were greeted in the Jazz Section's office, which was squeezed into the upstairs of a suburban house. Posters covered the walls. The shelves and racks above our heads were crammed with publications on the living theatre, Dada, minimalist art and surrealist photography. Avant-garde articles, said Srp, were allowed under Musicians' Union rules, as long as they were strictly cultural. He operated a policy of meticulous adherence to the law. So far, this had ensured the Section's survival. But a month ago the police had ransacked the premises and removed the correspondence with the Ministry of Culture. If he was brought to trial he would no longer have the evidence to support his side of the case. The police also took the account books, making it virtually impossible to collect subscriptions. Opening a cupboard door, Srp proudly showed me his own bound volumes of American jazz magazines of the '20s and '30s. These at least had not been confiscated.

We walked to the nearest metro to find a safer place to talk, descending by stair and escalator to reach the A line deep in the bowels of the system. For an hour we travelled back and forth, sitting among the nondescript passengers. I was haunted by the smooth drawling vowels of the unnaturally soothing female tannoy announcer – 'Malostranska...aaa', 'Mala...aaa Strana...aaa', 'Leniiiiinovaaa', 'Strasnicka...aaa' and her soft, clipped staccato 'Mustek!' and 'Namesti Miru!' Srp told me how the Section kept going. The cost of mailing newsletters was paid out of the committee's own pockets but the additional expense of mailing other literature was too much for them. Many country members had been travelling up to the office in Prague, deeply offended at being labelled 'hostile elements'. The Section's concerts in Prague's music clubs were now spoiled by plain clothes policemen mingling with the crowd, making notes of names and taking photographs. House searches followed, sometimes arrests. Alternative venues were being sought in garages or private houses. 'We are not anti-Government,' said Srp. 'We even send records of our music to President Husák. What they are doing to us is like using tanks to crush butterflies.'

Together we planned how I could help if the arrests came. My eyes were continually caught by Srp's troubled, courageous stare, as if he were willing me to grasp the importance of the principles at stake, to commit myself to seeking out every line of international influence to procure the survival of the Jazz Section. How could I not agree? Of course … yes … on my return I would do what we had done for Father Popiełuszko. I would find a British lawyer who would fly to Prague and familiarise himself with the Section's case and what passed for the legal system in Czechoslovakia. If Srp was brought to trial, the lawyer would record the proceedings and we would alert the international press. With a final grasp of my hand, he made his farewell. 'If I go to prison, make contact with Dr Průša, my lawyer. Raise money for my family.' His words would remain with me during his long ordeal in the months ahead.

I found Petr Rezek at home. We went up the road to a bar I had not seen before and had a long drink at an outside table. Neither of us referred to our awkward contretemps a year before. Instead, he cheerfully filled me in on the next chapter of his life story. He had not spent much time with his students because of his Plotinus translation, which he was trying to finish before the birth of his baby in December. His wife and he were both pleased about her pregnancy. Indeed she wanted to remarry him, but Petr preferred to remain divorced. It was the only way to keep his second flat.

Once his Plotinus was completed, Rezek aimed to puncture the reverential attitude of Prague's intellectuals – especially Radim Palouš – towards Patočka. They were turning him into a biblical prophet. To restore a sense of proportion, Rezek would bring together Patočka's early essays and some new unpublished ones, to which he would provide a critical commentary.

The next day was Pavel Bratinka's day off from boiler duties. I set off early, taking the subway to the east of Prague. Bratinka met me at the door and led me to a dark sitting room with a high ceiling. Seeing my surprise that he was able to live in a spacious apartment with several rooms, he explained that his father-in-law was a Party *apparatchik*. That must also have been why he had never been arrested.

He spoke of recent events in Moravia, none of which had reached the Western press, delivering the story in that individual style of his which conveyed the sense of colour and majesty that the occasion deserved. It left a strange music in my memory. On 7 July half a million people had come together for the eleven hundredth anniversary of the death of St Methodius, patron saint of the Slavs. Tens of thousand of pilgrims had camped overnight to hear Cardinal Tomášek say mass. Alone among the dissidents, Bratinka understood the scale of the seismic change that was occurring and would end in the collapse of European Communism. 'The cracks grow daily,' he said. 'There was no fear. For the first time the roles of crowd and police were reversed. It was the crowd who were in control, while the police were reduced to mere onlookers.'

Bratinka was pleased to have elicited from me a promise to lure Norman Podhoretz, the editor of *Commentary*, to Prague. He greatly admired Podhoretz for his courage in standing up to the political correctness that was sweeping across America's intelligentsia. Each month Bratinka would wait in anticipation for the next issue of *Commentary* to reach the American Embassy. I warned him semi-jokingly that Podhoretz might prove a disappointment in the flesh. Writers who were brave in print often turned to jelly when faced with the realities of a day or two behind the Iron Curtain. Apropos of that, 'How did Professor Hale's visit go?' Bratinka asked. He had heard that there had been a problem. There had indeed. Sir John Hale had been meant to give a talk on the Italian Renaissance two weeks before at Hejdánek's seminar. Distinctly nervous at the accounts he had heard of a crackdown, he had muddled up the date, arriving the wrong week. His subsequent report told the rest:

Hejdánek was surprised to see me, as he had been told that I'd be speaking on the previous Thursday. Would I stay and talk there and then to his group, which was beginning to assemble? I said that I'd rather get settled into the Panorama Hotel. He agreed and invited me for the following day. At about 6.15 pm, while I was changing before setting off for the meeting, a knock at the door, and three men who said they were police and showed me their I.D.s. I invited them in and their spokesman said that it would be very unwise of me to go to Mr Hejdánek's; if I wished to lecture I should not have pretended to be a tourist and should have approached Charles University. I said that that would be 'work' and I was on holiday. What I was going to give was an informal talk to a small circle of friends on a non-political topic. Surely the constitution guaranteed Czech citizens the right to learn. He said that if I insisted I would find my visit terminated in a not very happy way.

Early next morning I went to Hejdánek to apologise; I had come to feel that I had put personal convenience above a more important gesture of solidarity. He said (possibly to ease my guilt) that as more police had come the previous evening and taken names, it was probably better that I did not come. When I asked how the police had known of my talk, he shrugged and said he supposed that either his apartment was bugged or there was an informer in the group. I left Prague with a troubled conscience and a deep concern for the victims of thought-policing.

Bratinka pondered the Hale story sympathetically. 'We do not give enough recognition to the effort of will it takes to visit us,' he said, coming as close as he ever would to paying me a compliment. 'Nevertheless, you will bring Norman Podhoretz here, will you not?' He had another request, too. He wanted the Jan Hus to persuade the International Federation of Lawyers to issue a statement about a man who had been sentenced to gaol for saying prayers with children at a summer camp. I took away with me his legal commentary on the case. As usual, I was concerned about the risk of being searched at the border, but Bratinka had a novel suggestion. He had developed a good relationship with Dennis Keefe at the British Embassy – they were in the habit of driving out of Prague to pick mushrooms together, generally followed by three black cars with smoked windows. Could I ask Keefe to send material through the diplomatic bag?

My conversations at the British Embassy usually took place out of doors, except for those with the ambassador, who preferred to communicate by passing notes. I met Dennis Keefe in the garden. He agreed to give messages to Bratinka if they arrived in the diplomatic bag, but not if they had been sent through unofficial channels. As for the flow in the other direction or the transmission of documents to London – that was up to the ambassador: it was too big a decision for Keefe to take on his own.

My most sensitive material was a comprehensive summary of Brno *samizdat*. The ambassador said cautiously that he would take twenty-four hours to determine what protocol would allow him to do. I suppressed the irritated thought that information of such quality should have been required reading for the entire Czech desk and that the Embassy should have considered itself privileged to have access to it. Next day the ambassador agreed to send the *samizdat*, but added pointedly that this was an exception that would not be repeated. The bag was reserved for official business. Change or no change in the mood at 10 Downing Street, I was not to trouble him again.

Hoping for a less chilly diplomatic reception, I went on to see the American ambassador Bill Luers, who invited me to stay for lunch with his wife Wendy, a tough-looking New Yorker with a supercharged air. Bratinka's *samizdat* was not to the Luers' taste. They mistrusted the conservative ideas that attracted him. Nonetheless, as I got to know Wendy Luers I liked her and thought we would become friends. In the end, however, politics got in the way. Our perceptions of artistic life in Czechoslovakia were incompatible. Wendy was quite an authority on state-licensed painting, and had been taken in by the fiction that no Czechs were barred from exhibiting their work. Blissfully ignorant about those who were excluded from the system, she was affronted by a piece about the cultural scene in Brno that I showed her in draft.

I had had great difficulty reaching Charlie. I had tried unsuccessfully to call him from Brno and now I tried again from a call box with Alena Hromádková, whom I had caught up with a few hours before she was due to leave town. Still no luck. Suddenly I was losing concentration and wanted to get home as soon as I could.

There was one more day to get through and I forced myself to make a last call. Petr Pithart's success in having an article published in *The Times* had given him unrealistic ideas. I tried to discourage him from expecting too much from his ambition to write a monthly 'Letter from Prague'. But my mind was elsewhere. For once it was an unqualified relief to be on the flight to Heathrow.

Mrs Thatcher made her farewell to Charlie by inviting us to lunch at Chequers. To get Charlie out of the car and up the wide steps to the front door was a time-consuming operation and I was grateful that the Thatchers waited for some time in the drawing room before welcoming us in. We lunched in an alcove overlooking the lawn. Over coffee afterwards, with Denis taking a nap beside us on the sofa, we fell to discussing the impending Cabinet reshuffle. What did Charlie think of X? Should she invite Y back? One by one she sought his opinion on the Cabinet and their potential replacements. After we left, Mrs Thatcher behaved as if he was to be around for a long time. 'I look forward with confidence to the great things you have in store,' she wrote. 'I just wish that there were more people like you...'

In October, Charlie was in hospital for the last time. Right up to the end he continued to write his leaders and edit the paper. My friend Christine Stone remembers a telephone discussion with him about an article she had drafted a few days before his death – one of the first to highlight the Jazz Section and Petr Oslzlý's Theatre on a String, then on tour in Bristol. Charlie encouraged me to go and see Oslzlý, but I was anxious not to be away from London for more than a few hours and agreed to meet him halfway, at our house in Gloucestershire, during an afternoon break in the show. I waited in vain for an hour at Swindon station. Just as he was leaving his hotel to catch the train, he had been waylaid by his Party minder. It was out of the question to explain where he was going, so he had missed the train and had been obliged to take a taxi. Getting home just as Oslzlý arrived, I promptly put him on a horse and took him for a long ride – something he had not done since childhood. When he went on stage in *Commedia dell'Arte* that night – a fast-moving show of acrobats, duels and flaming torches – his bent figure and stiff hobble attracted suspicion, though he never revealed where he had been. Meanwhile, with a heavy heart, I drove back through the night to London.

A few days later I was alerted by the doctors that Charlie was fading, with only days, possibly hours, to live. I collected Tara and Luke from school and drove them to the hospital to say goodbye to their father. Charlie's mother, sister and close friends followed; others wrote before the end to tell him of their feelings for him. He died on 29 October 1985.

Twelve

Radio Free Europe beamed out the news of Charlie's death throughout Eastern Europe. Its director, George Urban, held a one-minute silence in his office. The last visitor of the year to go to Czechoslovakia was our trustee Paul Flather. He wrote: 'I passed on the sad news about Charles Douglas-Home to everybody whom I met. All sent Jessica their sincerest condolences. Alena was particularly upset as Jessica had been with her when trying to contact C D-H. She sent a present by return beautifully wrapped – later to be taken by the secret police.'

During Charlie's three-year illness I had searched in vain for some spiritual understanding of his ordeal. Even the Book of Job failed me. Amid my loneliness and tears I was often visited by anger that he had been allotted so much suffering and so short a life. The news that now reached me would have upset me at the best of times, but in my present fragile state it was too much for me. Towards the end of his mission Paul Flather had been arrested at the Austrian border and his notebook and address book had been removed. His coding had been flimsy. He had messages for Kavan as well as the Jan Hus. The secret police would have a lot to go on.

Throughout that gloomy, fog-bound November and December, my fears for Alena, Bratinka, Petr Pithart and the Brno people tormented me. Roger had gone to San Francisco in September for a six-month sabbatical at Stanford. Telephone calls from California produced little more than increased anxiety at both ends of the line. The rest of the trustees discussed the problem inconclusively. There was no visible avenue of damage limitation. All we could do was send a messenger to Prague, a student who would not be known to the secret police. We heard how each of our friends in turn had listened quietly and sadly, receiving the news in silence. Now they could only wait.

Paul's recollection of what he had written down was vague. I tried to calm myself with the thought that the secret police must have been tracking most of our contacts for a long time and there was not much that they could do to the known dissidents that they had not already done. Word came, however, that Petr Oslzlý had been picked up, interrogated and barred from travelling abroad. This was a body blow for Theatre on a String and for Oslzlý personally, but at least his connection with Jiří Müller had not been given away. Knowing that a visit from me at this stage could do no good and might even do harm, I went to ground in Gloucestershire, hoping against hope that there would be no more reprisals.

Charlie's memorial service in St Paul's Cathedral was organised by Rupert Murdoch – I was not up to doing it myself. The boys, now sixteen and fourteen, bore themselves courageously during the service, at which Alfred Brendel played one of Charlie's favourite pieces by Beethoven – the adagio from the D-minor sonata. For several months I received twenty or so letters a day – deeply expressed messages of affection or admiration from Charlie's friends all over the world, among them reminders of the influence of his writing in tributes from Mrs Thatcher and President Reagan.

My brother Martin perceptively recalled our nineteen-year marriage and advised me with the insight of an elder brother not to react to Charlie's death by undertaking some impulsive action but to 'defer it until you have discussed it thoroughly with people you think would be likely to <u>disagree</u> with you the <u>most</u>'. The nurse who had looked after Charlie just before he died wrote: 'I feel I was fortunate to have nursed Charlie. During the long nights he often spoke of death and dying to me. Often his pain could be relieved by sitting with him, and listening to parts of Mozart's requiem which appeared to give him peace of mind. We shall always remember him with affection. Some of us were able to love him too. I hope we were able to be of some comfort to him during his long illness.' Through these letters I gradually began to regain my strength.

In May 1986 Russia's nuclear plant at Chernobyl split and came close to meltdown. As the wind bore the lethal radioactive clouds north-west from the Ukraine over Poland towards Scandinavia, urgent radio appeals were broadcast to stay indoors and not to drink water or eat fresh vegetables. The European Community announced a ban on food imports from the affected area. I rang Warsaw to find that Małgorzata and Marcin Król were keeping their two young children back from school. In districts that had been particularly badly affected, we sent our friends iodine pills to counteract the effects of radiation. For the first time I felt able to be involved again.

One morning in June I received a slip of paper through the post, forwarded by Timothy Garton Ash. It was from five artists in Budapest who called themselves Inconnu, the Unknown. The leader of Inconnu, Sándor Szilágyi, invited Western artists to submit paintings for an exhibition to mark the thirtieth anniversary of the Hungarian Revolution. By reputation Hungary had grown considerably richer and freer than the other Soviet satellite countries, but I had not been there and wanted to see for myself. This was an opportunity to go, in the same way that I had first gone to Poland, through a chance invitation by a total stranger.

At first Roger flatly refused to take on another Eastern European country. Almost all of his free time was absorbed by Czechoslovakia and Poland, and he was simultaneously teaching at Birkbeck College, editing the *Salisbury Review*, writing another book on philosophy and touring the country giving lectures. Nevertheless, in August 1986 he was tempted to accompany me to Budapest for a few days. What finally persuaded him was that he was spared any preparatory work: I had lined up the addresses of an interesting selection of dissident writers and artists. But I had made an exception to our normal rule of confining ourselves to the underground movement – I planned a surprise call on Andras Hegedus, a Communist cadre of thirty years ago who by an accident of history had been cast into a central role in the great uprising of 1956.

Between the wars Hungary had been a country of violent political extremes. When the German tanks entered Russia in 1941 the Hungarian Government allied itself with the conqueror, but when the war turned and the Red Army overran the country, a ruthless group of Moscow-trained activists followed in its wake. Over the next few years the Hungarian Communist Party systematically liquidated its opponents. The last hope for democracy was lost when the Catholic Cardinal Mindszenty was tortured into a confession of treason and the 'good Communist' Rajk was executed. Under Rakosi, Hungary descended into a pit of terror.

In 1956, three years after his death, Stalin was denounced by the new Soviet leader Nikita Khrushchev. At last the Hungarians detected a ray of hope and in October a student revolution broke out all over the country, soon joined by every section of the population. After a few weeks of indecision Khrushchev sent tanks and Mongol troops to crush the uprising and murder its heroes, among them Prime Minister Imre Nagy.

Andras Hegedus had been Nagy's predecessor, a nonentity installed by the Kremlin. It was to him that the students had first come with their naive demands for elementary freedoms. In the bloodshed that followed he slunk out of the country to safety in Moscow, but he had since returned.

We found him on a sweltering hot day in the apricot orchard of his little house in a leafy suburban street above the castle of Buda. At his garden gate we had pressed the bell and waited. We were about to leave when we heard footsteps. Turning, we saw a small, round, old man with a greying moustache, wearing a brown aertex shirt. His full cheeks and balding top gave his face the look of a genial farmer, though something in his moist grey eyes – unless it was my imagination – spoke of the crimes in which he had once been an accomplice. With quiet courtesy he apologised for not coming earlier to the gate – he had thought it was unlocked. Then he led us up the path and into the house, beckoning us forward with gentlemanly concern.

We entered the living room, in which there was a rather good 1920s Hungarian painting of a village scene. The walls were lined with political and economic books, mostly in Hungarian, but with some English and Russian titles. In an English that was far from secure he offered us coffee, then padded out to order it from an old and secret wife. There was a red telephone on his desk and a pile of manuscripts on the sofa.

I told him we were thinking of arranging a conference to celebrate the thirtieth anniversary of the uprising. He was immediately interested, anxious to be invited. He began to discuss dates and potential formats for the event. Then he fell into reminiscence, telling us how his views had changed; he was evidently well pleased to be labelled a revisionist. He praised the work of the Czech reform movement, spoke well of Leszek Kolakowski and showed us an English journal, *Communism Today,* in which his own thoughts were discussed. In his opinion Nagy had made three 'mistakes' in 1956: his declaration of neutrality, his announcement that Hungary would withdraw from the Warsaw Pact, and his promise of a multi-party system with free elections. Hegedus's dead phraseology reduced Nagy's dramatic actions, which would have terminated Hungarian Communism and ripped a hole in the Soviet bloc, to a banal series of tactical miscalculations.

Once or twice he gestured to the manuscripts. They contained his memoirs, which were soon to be published. He was very proud of them and anticipated a kind of delayed vindication. Always he was soft-spoken, gentle, with a little twinkle in his peasant eyes. Yet sometimes when he looked at me he seemed to be making a cold assessment of my presence. I was struck by his absorption in the affairs of Hungary – his land-locked, time-bound sense that whatever had mattered in the world had mattered because the wheels of history were once active *here* and *through him*. We left him with cordial hand-shakes and insincere plans for future contact.

Our waiting taxi drove away from Hegedus's bourgeois area of the city, past the rock-face of Buda, down to the narrow roads between the hill and the west bank of the Danube. We crossed over the long bridge into the wide tree-lined boulevards of the Paris-style quarter of Pest. With a sense of excitement I saw that this part of the city was unrestored and uncontaminated by concrete, glass, steel or high-rise towers. At eye-level the grey stucco of the crumbling façades was pockmarked and gashed with bullet holes – a legacy of the street fighting of 1945 and 1956. Large wooden doors under disintegrating lintels opened off the pavement into hidden courtyards.

Our destination was Gabor Demský, reputed to be the most active of the *samizdat* editors. Demský lived in the attic of a dignified four-storey stone house where he presided over an antique desk in a low, dark room crammed with books, pamphlets and leaflets. I peered at the titles. His publications revealed his personal horizons as surprisingly insular compared with those of the Czech and Polish underground editors. Without exception the authors were Hungarian – no Hayek, no Popper, no Solzhenitsyn, not a trace of European philosophy or literature.

It was an illusion, he told us, that Hungarians were less constrained than other Eastern Europeans. There might be more freedom to travel and more liberal access to international art and literature, but genuine protest that challenged the political *status quo* was as harshly dealt with as anywhere else behind the Iron Curtain. A new law had been passed under which editors could receive heavy fines for publishing ideas in conflict with 'the consensus'. For some trifling transgression, 1,500 copies of a scholarly journal had recently been seized and pulped. *Samizdat* editors lived under constant surveillance and were frequently raided.

Demský was not enthusiastic about our proposals of exchanges with Western academics. So far as he was concerned, Hungarian intellectuals were mainly interested in their own ideas. Where we could help was in supplying his publishing organisation with the paper-cutting, stapling and glueing equipment he found so hard to obtain in Hungary. I was not entirely convinced that Demský was representative of Hungarian dissident thinking. Nevertheless, his negativeness and his narrow concentration on the domestic scene came as something of a relief. We would have been hard put to mount an effective operation in a new country.

As dusk fell, the streets of Budapest were deserted. We had twice tried unsuccessfully to ring Sándor Szilágyi, but now we found him at home, a slim, short and handsome thirty-year-old, with a sensitive face and a direct gaze. Although he had had no notice of our visit, he received us as if our arrival were the most natural event imaginable. His apartment was devoid of furniture except for a 1930s stove which stood on tiptoe on four curled feet in a corner. The steel cooking ring trickled out gas under a flimsy tin jug in which we brewed dark coffee, which we poured ritualistically over and over again into small china cups. The drug-like effect of the caffeine was heightened by lack of food. Sitting ravenous on the bare boards, we fell into an intense discussion of contemporary Hungarian life.

Szilágyi was, it seemed, an impresario as much as an artist, orchestrating a group of painters and poets while keeping himself afloat with a menial job. The group led a nomadic existence, exhibiting their art and reading their poems in friends' apartments, in empty buildings, sometimes in the street. Szilágyi himself was a master of elusiveness. By the time the police arrived at the premises, everybody had always vanished. Hence their name, Inconnu.

The anniversary of the Revolution was an occasion to solicit support from the West. Szilágyi had sent a manifesto to the *New York Review of Books*, which had passed it to Timothy Garton Ash, but so far the only response was our unannounced knock on the door. I sifted through his material with interest. None of it was of very high quality, but Inconnu's badges, signs, posters and graphics gave a recognisable visual character to the Hungarian opposition, modelled on Solidarity's logo, which six years earlier had imprinted itself on the world's imagination with its blood-red dancing letters hoisting the national flag aloft.

The superficial Western assumption that Hungary was almost democratic, or at any rate reasonably open and prosperous, irritated Szilágyi. Like Demský, he believed there was little to choose between the satellite countries. The one-party system, the controlled press, the sham parliament, the almost universal state ownership and the obedience to Moscow, these were the shared marks of the Soviet empire everywhere. Had it not been for Western credits, he believed that there might well have been another Hungarian revolution. I was sceptical. To a visitor accustomed to the constant watchfulness of Poland and Czechoslovakia, Hungary appeared markedly less oppressed – and the idea of a second revolution in such a deflated atmosphere struck me as fanciful.

Two big local issues were preoccupying dissident circles. The first concerned the building of a dam. A twenty-five-mile stretch of the Danube was to be diverted into a concrete canal, depriving vast tracts of agricultural land of natural irrigation. The beneficiaries would be the Czechs, who were to receive a hydroelectric plant. A Hungarian protest group calling itself the Danubian Circle had formed. This even contained some prominent members of the Academy of Sciences.

The second issue was the deteriorating relationship with Romania. In 1947 western Transylvania, with its still largely Hungarian population, had been returned to Romania. This upheaval had been mitigated by guarantees that Hungarian-speaking schools, media and cultural organisations could keep their own language. However, all traces of Transylvania's Hungarian past were now being erased. The last radio station had been closed in 1985. Hungarian names were being written out of the history books; and Hungarian tombstones were being changed to Romanian. The final insult came when 20,000

Hungarian-language bibles, sent to churches in Transylvania by American Christians, were turned into lavatory paper under Ceauşescu's orders. The failure of Prime Minister Kadár to speak up for Hungary's compatriot minority across the border served as a reminder that he was no more than a puppet of the Kremlin.

Before we left Budapest we called on a number of other dissidents. But we found no unifying theme, nothing that could be described as an alternative culture. The dissidents were full of pessimism. They seemed to us to be too factional and too focused on the goal of travel in the West to benefit from the sort of programmes that we had set up for the Czechs and Poles. We reflected ruefully that Demský had been right to be discouraging. The only one among them who had an appetite for our broader approach was Iván Bába, who was from the Hungarian minority in Slovakia. Bába was the leading light of a group that claimed to speak for the countryside. He was not immune from the Hungarian disease of internecine bickering, but along with a fierce sense of nationhood he had an awareness of the need to connect with international streams of civilisation.

In the back of our minds – mine at any rate – the fantastic idea had been forming that if only the satellite countries could act in concert they might free themselves from the Soviet grip. The demoralised self-obsession of the Hungarians was depressing, but not enough to deter us from trying to organise a *samizdat* convention in Budapest, where editors from all over Eastern Europe could meet. We returned to Hungary twice on planning missions, but in the end the convention came to nothing, thwarted by Czech and Polish visa problems. We did, however, manage to set up a Polish-Hungarian conference in Vienna, chiefly memorable for Roger's acerbic comments on the dreary neo-Marxist contributions of the Hungarians, who had been forced to submit their papers for domestic censorship. Meanwhile, we sent books and cartridges of photocopier ink for Demský, Bába and Inconnu.

When the historian Norman Davies went out he summarised the scene in his report:

I spent two days in Budapest, mainly with Ivan Bába. It was a valuable experience for me to contrast the predicament of the Hungarian opposition, which struggles for minimal support in a relatively prosperous but effectively repressed society, with the much larger and stronger opposition in Poland. . . . I hope it was worthwhile for them to discuss matters of common interest such as Hungary/Poland relations and the Transylvanian problem compared to Poland's 'lost territories' in the East: the Jewish question: and the (deplorable) state of Sovietology in Britain and America. I was able to deliver a cartridge (fondled but not opened by a customs man at the airport).

Despite Bába's and Sandor Szilágyi's pleas, in the end we reluctantly decided not to form a separate trust for Hungary, but to deal with specific cases through a sub-section of the Polish Jagiellonian Foundation. I took a special interest in the work of Inconnu. I wrote about the group in the *Spectator* and sent letters to artists who might be sympathetic, asking them to lend a painting for the exhibition to commemorate the uprising. No reply came from Lucian Freud – whose Viennese roots I had hoped might stir him to generosity – but five others produced paintings and drawings.

I found it oddly inspiring to be commissioned for a painting. David Pryce-Jones's account of street fighting in his *Hungarian Revolution 1956* gave me the idea for a large gouache in burnt umber, yellow ochre and cerulean blue. I sketched out a dark-coated solitary figure clutching a gun, himself under fire, crouched in front of a large window on the top floor of a Budapest apartment building. Shafts of near-white sunlight fell in geometrical streaks onto an iron bed, floorboards and slabs of broken wall. The window's rectangular frame, blasted into the room by a tank shell, swung towards the man's right shoulder. Nothing among these zig-zagging lines was irrevocably destroyed; each part waited to return intact to its original place.

Eventually I collected up six paintings, delivering them by car to the London flat of a dissident exile, George Krassó. He took them in a suitcase to Budapest. Predictably, the police raided the exhibition and none of the paintings was ever seen again.

Thirteen

For at least eighteen months we had anticipated the net closing on Karel Srp. In the hope that Norman St John Stevas might stave off the authorities, we supplied him with a mass of telling detail. He used this to good effect at the Cultural Forum in Budapest. But his speech, denounced by Hungarian radio as 'an ideological onslaught on the Soviet Union', was lost among thirty-five bland statements from other countries. The bit now between his teeth, St John Stevas went on to Prague, where he met Srp ostentatiously in a café before attending appointments with Party *apparatchiks*.

On 2 September 1986, evidently tiring of their cat and mouse game, the authorities pounced on Srp and six other committee members of the Jazz Section, holding them in custody on the charge of running an illegal commercial enterprise. Srp, as chairman, faced an additional charge of illegal financial dealings. The maximum sentence for these offences was eight years.

As soon as we heard the news we went into action. We had prepared a number of writers for the impending arrests and a barrage of articles appeared in rapid succession. In the *New York Times*, the novelist Kurt Vonnegut described the Czech authorities as 'cannibalistic Forces of Satan'. Norman Podhoretz, who had finally summoned up the courage to go to Prague and had been much affected by his meetings with Bratinka, wrote a long and highly emotional piece for the *Washington Post*. Tom Stoppard and Kingsley Amis signed a joint letter to *The Times* urging Britain to sever diplomatic relations with Czechoslovakia. There was scarcely a newspaper of authority that did not carry a strong article or editorial.

The next move was to put a lawyer into play. Geoffrey Robertson, one of London's most prominent QCs, had already fought several high profile trials, having defended Michael X on death row in Trinidad and saved a missionary from the firing squad in Mozambique. Czechoslovakia might be a tempting new challenge to such an inveterate traveller, with a taste for the exotic and no aversion to publicity. In his crowded diary Robertson managed to free up an October weekend in Prague. A smuggled letter from Jiří Müller, sent in reply to mine, arrived a week before he left. 'You were even quicker than we were. I'm not certain if we can ensure success of visit but we'll do our best ...the lawyer should take the airport bus (not taxi) to the centre, then underground to Kačerov to see Jaroslav Korčán who will brief him...towards the end of the day an "accidental" meeting with Havel. Your lawyer should be prepared for this.'

The visit started badly when Dr Průša, the lawyer responsible for the Jazz Section's legal strategy, missed the initial meeting. Průša had been detained for questioning for seven hours by the police, not because they knew of his appointment with Robertson but because of a demonstration by a few Jazz Section members outside their closed headquarters. He was in any event a marked man. He had won a golden reputation for defending dissidents and had served a five-year sentence for 'perverting justice', at the same time as Václav Havel's imprisonment. Robertson saw his value and recommended that we pay him a fee for advising witnesses on their rights. As a form of protection Robertson also arranged for Průša to become a member of the International Bar Association.

Robertson understood perfectly the essentials of the totalitarian judicial process. Legality was a myth of the state's making. The law had no standing, judges no independence; justice consisted of the will of the Party. There had, however, been some cosmetic developments '...Communist governments had by this time', he wrote later, 'learned to deflect international concern about human rights by pretending that dissidents were imprisoned for real crimes rather than for their thoughts ... The case against the Jazz Section executives was announced to the world as a fraud case, but this was itself a fraud: the Section was strictly non-profit, staffed entirely by unpaid volunteers.'

On his return, Robertson brought back a letter for Charles Alexander at the International Jazz Federation, noting in his report to us: 'Alexander's conduct is crucial to the defence strategy, which is based on the continuing legality of the Section through its affiliation with the International Association. He must be in a position to say he knows their names and recognises their legitimacy.' We were anxious about Alexander's reaction. He had accepted that the Section should not be expelled from the Federation, but he had been taking the line that his ability to help was restricted by concern for the damage that might be done to artists in other Communist countries. His own sources, such as they were, had told him that the reports about impending trials and imprisonment were fiction. Would he stick his neck out now that the crisis had come? To our great relief he did, committing the Federation to full support.

Our next step was to organise a petition. The composer David Matthews took on the task of explaining to celebrities from the worlds of pop, jazz and classical music why the release from custody of seven unknown members of an unknown Czech club was important. It was never going to be easy to agree a text with swinging figures of left and right such as Bob Geldorf, Sting, Andrew Lloyd Webber, Pete Townshend, Nigel Kennedy and Elton John, as well as with respected veterans such as Michael Tippett, Ronnie Scott and Lennox Berkeley, but the path was smoothed by a judicious resort to political correctness. 'We write', we said solemnly, 'in the spirit of friendship for Czechoslovakia.' Paul McCartney added his name, together with a drawing of a smiling face and a message: 'Best wishes to all Czech musicians!!' By December David Matthews had collected fifty-eight names. On Christmas Eve, with a full press fanfare, the petition was delivered to the Czech Embassy. The following day the Czech Senate announced a postponement of the Section's preliminary hearing.

The Czech Party's indecision was perhaps heightened by Gorbachev's recent release of the dissident nuclear physicist Andrei Sakharov from his exile in Gorky. They were not sure from what direction the political wind was blowing. On the other hand, it was equally possible that the case had merely been withdrawn temporarily from the limelight until the Western media found a different story to chase. In any event, the saga was likely to continue for a long time yet and we were running out of money. I had promised Srp that we would look after the families of the arrested and keep up the political pressure if he went to prison. It seemed to me that Americans had the strongest tradition of giving generously to causes which awakened their moral convictions. So I flew to New York to try my luck with some small foundations which I knew of only by name. The Smith Richardson Foundation gave us £12,000 and Helsinki Watch £1,000. I doubt these charities ever did more good for less money: and even now I wonder whether they realise quite how much their contributions meant.

During the eighteen months since his defection, Hubka's problems had gone from bad to worse. For a time he had been kept going by the business of acquiring British asylum and starting a new life. Roger Scruton procured him a temporary fellowship at Birkbeck and a research post at Westfield – two colleges attached to London University. But the grant we had obtained for him was not renewable. He was unable to find a permanent university job and became disillusioned and depressed.

Earlier in the year Roger had received out of the blue a packet of Home Office correspondence posted from West Berlin. Without telling any of us, Hubka had decided to return to Czechoslovakia. His presumed intention in sending his papers to Roger was to leave his asylum application in safe hands, in case things went badly for him. At the border he had been turned away by the Czech police and told that he would not be allowed back to his country.

For two months Hubka soldiered on in London. Then one day he threw himself from an upstairs window of his seedy Bayswater bed-and-breakfast. The first we heard about his death was when Roger was called by the police, who had found his number in Hubka's telephone book. In late summer 1986 I arranged the funeral in the Carmelite church in Kensington. Hard as I tried, nobody would come, for he had made few friends in England. Bamber Gascoigne gave a moving address to a pitiful congregation of four: '... It is a symptom of his tragedy that his funeral should take place so far away from those who knew him best, and loved him most. ... Although it was the appeal of freedom, in particular academic freedom, that had brought Karel to England, he soon came to feel that this freedom was hollow without his family, perhaps even that he needed his family more than his freedom.'

To this day I have not been able altogether to shake off a feeling of guilt. We all asked ourselves whether, had we tried harder, we might somehow or other have found Hubka a way of supporting himself. We had done our utmost to dissuade him from defecting. His scholarship did not reach the standard for a university career and he was adamant in refusing to set his sights lower. We even had some grounds for resentment, for the manner of his death caused ill-informed gossip to the effect that we were partly responsible for it. The truth was that ultimately he, too, was the victim of a system which forced him to choose between servitude at home and a desolate freedom abroad, where he could find neither work nor self-respect.

A message came from Hubka's widow Eva that she wanted his ashes smuggled back to Czechoslovakia, not returned through Czech officials' hands. By January 1987 there were so many pressing problems to resolve in Czechoslovakia that I could delay a visit no longer. On arrival I went straight to Pavel Bratinka, who I was sure would have the right instincts as to what should be done. It would upset Eva to receive the ashes at her home, so we went together to meet her in a mutual friend's house. I gave her the urn and the text of Bamber's tribute. She was convinced that her husband had been mentally disturbed and despite her sorrow was in some ways relieved that he was no longer lonely and tormented. In the spring, with the help of a priest, she would open his father's grave and scatter the ashes inside.

Jiří Exner was standing in for Srp as chairman of the Jazz Section. I found him cautiously keeping the Prague office going, determined not to fall into the trap of 'illegal trading'. I promised that on my return I would set up a Friends of the Section with Charles Alexander.

I went on to Havel's flat, to take him the text of an interview he had held with a British journal, in which he had developed the theme that multinational corporations had a disturbing feature in common with totalitarian governments – a deadening lack of a human dimension. This sounded exaggerated to me, but I did not argue for long; and he disarmed me by confessing that his views were probably coloured by his lack of familiarity with Western society. Anyway, we had practical matters to discuss. I brought him up to date on what we were doing for Karel Srp and the Jazz Section and asked his advice about the younger generation of dissidents. He suggested several names and offered to make introductions. He also warned me that Petr Pithart, whom I was due to call on next, was going through a bad time, hating the ghetto life which his dissidence forced on him. To keep contact with the outside world Pithart was obliged to give tea parties in his wife's name – people who shunned him as a dinner guest would not object to meeting him casually in the afternoon.

I reached Brno after a three-and-a-half-hour journey on icy roads, the driver skidding the bus from side to side, one hand on the wheel and the other devoted to chain-smoking. Brno in January was not as cold as I had imagined, perhaps because I was pleasurably cocooned in the Oslzlýs' overheated flat. Petr took me early to the theatre that night. He had to be made up for his own leading part as a revolutionary in his production of *Prodaný a Prodaná* (The Bartered and the Bought) – a historical play about the composer Smetana's librettist Karel Sabina, who had become an informer for the Austrian police because it was the only way for him to earn enough to be a writer. I was the first to arrive. I watched the theatre filling up with young people. Ten minutes before the play started all the seats were taken, with standing at the back. The play's contemporary message was unmissable. In the last scene I had to stand up to see anything as the audience in front of me jumped onto their seats to cheer Petr's impassioned speech.

I could see immediately how good Oslzlý's company was. It was equally at home in literary theatre and in rougher popular theatre based on improvisation, gesture and mime. That night the two forms were combined. There was nothing pretentious or self-indulgent about his work. He chose his actors partly for their agility. Dancing, singing, acting and juggling all came easily to them and their extraordinary speed at scene-changing kept up a cracking pace.

I had a flash of pain that because of Paul Flather's arrest this mesmerising troupe was now confined to Czechoslovakia, cut off from the outside world and depriving Western audiences of a unique theatrical experience. Oslzlý himself was more philosophical about it than I was. He had worked out a sort of consolation for himself. He would increase the volume of seminars – 'If I can't go out into the world, then I will do everything I can to bring the world to me.'

I was due to give a lecture on painting. Before I went out to Brno Bamber Gascoigne had taken me to supper in London, where he had asked me with a slightly worried look what I would be talking about. When I told him my subject, he was visibly relieved. Evidently he had suspected me of planning to proselytise for Reaganite defence policy or Thatcherite economics. His anxiety had, however, given me the idea I was looking for. I would talk to the Brno painters about political art, in particular the German Expressionists.

Before the First World War an impresario called Herewath Walden had inspired an aggressive school of socially conscious artists – the Expressionists, whose harsh, dissonant colours and spiky images evoked the extremes of inequality in the glare and tension of German city life. On Petr Oslzlý's white sitting room wall I projected dark woodcuts by Käthe Kollwitz, ink drawings by Otto Dix. The Czech oppressor today was not the class system or the exploiting boss, but a more brutal apparatus posing as the liberator of the common man. The Brno painters had their own Walden in Oslzlý but they had been hesitant to tackle political subjects. Perhaps the Expressionist analogy would stir them to be more ambitious.

These painters were certainly not lacking in courage or ingenuity. Oslzlý took me to visit a banned photographer who was exhibiting in the top of a tall building in the suburbs. Another artist, also without a licence, showed us his thinly disguised political drawings masquerading as cartoons for children. He had built a press out of an old mangle and discarded pieces of zinc which he scratched, using drypoint techniques. The worn-down plate printed like an etching, without the need for acid.

Most important to their *amour propre* was that they had acquired an exhibition space of their own in a discount chemist shop with a sympathetic manager. The first show had gone well. The exhibiting artist, dressed in a white chemist's coat, stood behind the counter serving cut-price goods; a 'cellist played solemnly on the shop floor while the guests mingled with bemused ordinary customers looking for toothpaste and sticking plasters. Two uniformed policemen hovered outside. Abruptly at six o' clock one of the policemen came in. While the 'cellist zipped up her instrument the chemist announced 'We're closed now' and turned off the light.

The day before I left, Oslzlý took me to meet a curator who lived several hours out of Brno in what before the war had been the centre of the Batá shoe industry. Mr Batá had built an attractive estate of simple houses for his employees and had created a museum of Czech art. Now run down and neglected, the gallery was looked after by a man who cared passionately for his country's heritage and implored me to find museums in London with which he could correspond. As we walked in the loneliness of the large echoing rooms, filled with four centuries of Central European portraiture, still-lifes and landscapes, I gained a sense of the richness of the Bohemian and Moravian past.

We took a different route on our return, passing countless examples of Renaissance architecture. The town of Telc, which appeared nowhere in text books or travel books and was unknown in the West, was a jewel. In its centre were perhaps thirty or forty Renaissance buildings. The outskirts had none of the high-rise buildings or smoke-belching factories which disfigured other towns.

This journey of discovery was a reminder that for some time we had been pressing Jiří Müller to help us expand our underground lectures farther afield, to Ostrava and Olomouc. No volunteers had yet come forward; we heard that people were too frightened in Olomouc. Jiří had always said that it would be impossible to find another Petr Oslzlý, someone with a large enough personality to make space for others in his wake. Nor was there word from Bratislava in Slovakia, where Charlie had been arrested nearly twenty years ago. I knew that the country was mountainous and secluded. Its Catholic peasant population had always moved at a slower pace than its Austrian, Hungarian and Czech neighbours. Under the Austro-Hungarian Empire the Slovaks had had the almost unlearnable Hungarian language imposed on them, smothering the rise of a middle class. And while the Czechs belonged to the Austrian part of the empire, which had achieved universal male suffrage in 1901, Slovakia had remained undemocratic to the end. To penetrate this isolated world would give us a real sense of achievement.

I had returned to London by the time that the Jazz Section's trial finally started. The judge gave a conciliatory summing up and Srp was given a sixteen-month sentence, while the others received shorter or suspended sentences. Of course the charges were absurd, but we congratulated ourselves that without the international publicity we had generated the court would have been less lenient. Many years later we made a shocking discovery. When the secret police files were opened they revealed the astonishing fact that Srp himself had at one stage been an informer. None of our Czech friends had suspected him. In retrospect, however, we had to ask ourselves whether the whole trial had been some sort of elaborate play. Such was the nature of life behind the Iron Curtain.

In July we had good news from Slovakia, when Jan Čarnogorský contacted us through Petr Oslzlý. A lawyer who was later to become Slovakia's first prime minister, he was everything that we could have hoped for. Some years back, he had been dismissed from his employment as a state attorney for 'taking the same position as his clients'. Nowadays he supplemented his meagre wage as a driver by subscriptions raised from church congregations for the defence of religious dissidents. With a handful of friends he had recently started to hold philosophical seminars. These had naturally caught the attention of the secret police of Bratislava, who were more zealous, perhaps because they had fewer distractions, than their colleagues in Prague. Nevertheless, he and his group were willing to take the risk of opening up a line of communication to the West.

Bob Grant, the doughty Glasgow don, was the first to reach Bratislava:

> I spoke for more than an hour and a quarter. The audience was about 15 to 18 people. Sometimes Čarnogorský translated after every sentence: sometimes after every third or fourth. . . . The Prague audience are politically more sophisticated. In Bratislava the group are nearly all serious Catholics. They have to be told who people like Hayek are, let alone what they say.
>
> C. confirmed that highly specialised topics would not be a

good idea. The political orientation of the audience, he told me, was roughly West German mainstream, ranging from Social to Christian Democrats, with most of them inclining towards the rightwards end of the spectrum: I suppose they have some idea of the German political map from Austrian TV. They were genuinely puzzled by my presenting British conservatism in secular terms. I pointed out that our countrymen are notoriously heathen in point of religious doctrine or observance, yet also much inclined to a vague religiousness or civic piety (as shown by their resort to religious forms at the great crises of life), and backed this up by Lord Melbourne's quip that he was not a pillar of the church, but a buttress: 'he supported it from outside'. Here someone interrupted, only half-laughingly, with 'Then you will all go to hell.' I decided I should not have seemed so airy about the whole thing.

They are hungry for Western political and current affairs journalism. They fell on the journals that I had brought in as if they were gold dust, and bore off even the previous day's *Times*, *Telegraph* and *Spectator* in triumph.

There was one listener, I was told afterwards, who did not fit into the general pattern. This was Prof. Kusý, formerly Professor of Marxism at the University of B. and chief ideologist of the Slovakian Community Party. Like Waugh's Mr Prendergast, he had been destroyed by his 'doubts', and was not a Western-style socialist...While the discussion was going on C. was called away to his front door. The new arrival, who remained in the hallway, was an Ed Norman from the US Embassy in Prague...he had come to report on events in Prague, where Benda *et al* had just been house-searched and charged. The hearing had been in open court, in deference to Glasnost, but of course the standard technique had been adopted of packing the courtroom with Party members, so that no strangers could get in. But Norman and some other diplomats had kicked up a fuss and eventually been admitted.

Bob Grant's visit was in the autumn of 1987. I was envious of him, for I longed to know Slovakia. But for the moment I had to defer that experience. The timing conflicted with my first visit to Romania.

Fourteen

I had for years had in my mind an image of Romania – a land of vast plains, wooded mountains and the mysterious lagoons of the Danube delta. I had inherited from my father a few pre-war books that conjured up Romania's ancient peasant culture close to the Ukrainian border in the hills of the Maramureş, where families had worked their own land continuously for over a thousand years, living in strange wooden-tiled houses and worshipping a Christian God in equally strange wooden churches. Further east stood the churches of Bukovina, their outside walls brightly painted with biblical stories. A hundred miles to the south, in Transylvania, two hundred medieval Saxon villages orbited seven untouched medieval towns: this was the Siebenbürgen, whose German-speaking population had for centuries survived danger by retreating behind the massive walls of their fortified churches – churches whose sacred interiors contained painted pews and altarpieces fit to be compared with the triptychs of the Italian Renaissance. Then there was Bucharest. I could almost smell the oriental capital, a city teeming with whip-cracking coachmen, cultured Jewish traders, gypsies, Turks and latecomers from the Hapsburg Empire.

Most of Romania's light and colour must, I knew, have been obliterated, but perhaps something remained. The country had once possessed the most fertile soil in Eastern Europe, but as the peasants and farmers were stripped of their land and herded into collective farms, its agriculture had collapsed. When Ceauşescu took power in 1965, he completed the destruction of the economy with a series of ruinous showcase projects. Among his worst aberrations was the Danube canal.

The Danube flowed unconcernedly between free and enslaved countries, beginning as a trickle in the alpland of West Germany, then swelling into a broad expanse as it passed through Vienna, Bratislava, Budapest and Belgrade before forming the boundary between Romania and Bulgaria and finally emptying into the Black Sea. Upstream, the Slovaks were damming the river for electricity, desiccating great tracts of Hungarian land. Ceauşescu's canal, bypassing the delta and linking the Danube to the sea, had been built by gangs of slave labour from the gulags, working with shovels and bare hands. Goodness knows how many died, their bodies interred in the canal bed, before the project was completed in 1984. Now, after three shipping seasons, it was still devoid of traffic.

Obsessed with his ambition to pay off Romania's $10 billion foreign debt, Ceauşescu was ransacking the country's basic resources, exporting everything he could lay his hands on. In much of the country food shortages brought the population close to starvation. Then, towards the end of 1985, word of a new horror began to seep out. An earthquake in Bucharest eight years earlier had given Ceauşescu the pretext to 'modernise' the city. His programme was initially unadventurous, but as his megalomania grew, he saw that architecture could become a symbol of his power. There was talk of great boulevards leading to an oval-shaped square where a quarter of a million worshippers could pay homage to their leader below the steps of a palace more gigantic than anything yet built in the world. The rumours were fed by compulsory acquisitions of land and property over ever larger areas.

A letter in *The Times,* signed 'Sherban Cantacuzino', described the systematic destruction of monuments and entire historic quarters in Bucharest. At least six sixteenth- and eighteenth-century churches had already been razed to the ground. Cantacuzino, a naturalised British citizen and a descendant of the seventeenth- and eighteenth-century Romanian rulers, might have added that his family's ancient tombs were next in line for the bulldozer. His letter sealed my determination to go to Romania and I started looking for contacts.

There were surprisingly few Romanian exiles in London. One of them was the flamboyant and flirtatious Ion Raţiu, who was married to a Pilkington glass heiress. Raţiu's monthly broadsheet, *The Free Romanian,* published articles on Ceauşescu's corruption and kept alive the memory of the country's seizure in 1947 by Moscow-trained agitators backed by the Soviet Army. Raţiu was a gallant figure, but in the climate of the era, when Ceauşescu's dubious independence from the USSR gave him the status of honorary liberal, the *Free Romanian*'s stance was regarded by right-thinking people, if they noticed it at all, as a ludicrous throwback to a bygone world.

Another valuable contact was Doreen Berry, who had worked for the Romanian section of the BBC World Service for twenty years from the 1940s – and had helped make it an island of truth in an ocean of disinformation. She put me in touch with the head of department, Christian Mititelu, who had defected to the West in the late 1960s. Both Doreen and Christian were encouraging. Dennis Deletant, by contrast, at the School of East European Studies, was inclined to think that any external help given to Romanian dissidents would backfire.

The Romanian émigrés in France were more numerous. I dragged Roger off to Paris, where we learned that there was no organised underground opposition in Romania. It was ten years since the writer Paul Goma, taking his inspiration from Charter 77 in Czechoslovakia, had been expelled for criticising Ceauşescu in an open letter. President Carter infelicitously chose the time of his expulsion to invite Ceauşescu to the White House. There, in the fashion of the day, the President praised his guest's wisdom and moderation. The resulting sense of despair led to a mass exodus of potential Romanian dissidents to the West.

Those whom we met in Paris suggested a number of names of possible contacts in Romania. They dismissed Deletant's warnings that our missions might do more harm than good and urged me to go to Bucharest. By the end of three days I was thoroughly committed. Roger was intrigued, but adamant that Hungary was his last shot. So I set off alone.

My plane landed many hours late on the night of 23 September 1987 in Bucharest's Otopeni airport – a ramshackle, ill-lit, concrete structure. Since nobody but my mother and the Romanian visa section in Kensington knew my flight details, I was disconcerted by the sound of my name being called repeatedly around the dilapidated terminal; and even more so when I was located by a pretty and immaculately dressed young woman who presented me with red carnations 'to welcome my arrival' and instantly disappeared. Had the Romanian communities in Paris or London been infiltrated? Was this a Judas kiss to identify me to a distant watcher? Or was it merely a mark of recognition of my late husband's name? I never knew. It was typical of the mystery that was to envelop my every experience in Romania.

The chief purpose of my visit was to find the 78-year-old Professor Constantin Noica, who had recently been propelled into the political limelight through two books by his pupil Gabriel Liiceanu recording philosophical dialogues at Noica's country retreat. Tales of Noica's ascetic way of life had reached me from Romanian expatriates. Liiceanu portrayed him as a Socratic figure, self-critical and generous, seeking enlightenment through reading, meditation and dialectical discussion. His calm rejection of ambiguity, after years of lies and half-truths, gave Romanians a glimpse of another world. Liiceanu's books generated a ferment in Bucharest and enraged the authorities.

In Czechoslovakia, Poland and Hungary there had been a network of friendships to fall back on: in Romania I had to rely on second-hand introductions. This left me uneasy. However many times I had been assured by exiles that such-and-such a person would want to see me, I knew how changeable individual circumstances could be under Ceauşescu's reign of terror. There was the additional concern that the Third Directorate of the political police had enforced a decree that made it a criminal offence to talk to foreigners without filing a report.

Before I went in search of Noica I had a call to make in Bucharest. After a sleepless night I dressed inconspicuously and set out on foot up Calea Victoriei to the north-east sector of the city. If I were followed, I would have no difficulty in detecting my pursuer. There were so few people. Empty side streets, no stalls, no cafés, no bustle, no life. Where was everybody? Only two vans went by during my walk. Private cars had been banned in Bucharest since January.

I turned right into the wide main road of Boulevard Dacia, slipped through a courtyard into a block of flats, climbed a staircase to the first floor and steeled myself to knock on the door of Flat 15, marked Celac-Botez. I heard footsteps coming towards me; the door opened a crack; dark eyes met mine in a blank stare. I whispered the name of Michnea Berindei as introduction and was ushered in. Mariana Celac's soft-spoken welcome soothed my anxiety. In a subsequent pencil drawing I recorded my first impression of her sitting at her desk, her thick, straight haircut, with its heavy fringe, framing a wide face that exuded authority and intelligence. 'Her flat', I wrote afterwards in my diary, 'is a combination of all the ones I know belonging to dissidents, whether in Prague, Cracow, Brno or Budapest ... the same austere atmosphere ... a feeling of peace as if I had come home; the bookcases, the shelves, the desk, the darkness and lack of clutter, nothing on the walls except objects of intense significance.'

A few weeks earlier Mariana's husband, Mihai Botez, had left to make a new life in the United States. This was a disappointment, for as recently as May I had read an interview in the *Christian Science Monitor* in which he criticised those who fled the country: 'When dissidents protest, face persecution, and then leave for the West, the Goverment can say that we only want to get the better living conditions on the other side. If 1,000 of us intellectuals would stay then we would have an impact.' Three months after the article, however, he and his wife had come to a decision: as a mathematician of international repute, Mihai would emigrate to America, while Mariana, who felt that she would not be able to re-establish herself abroad as a practising architect, would stay behind to look after her mother. They had no children.

The last ten years had been a severe test of their endurance. They belonged to a generation which had been optimistic for the Ceauşescu regime in its early years, seeing in it a promise of modernisation and openness to Western ideas. The youngest Romanian ever to receive a doctorate in mathematics, Mihai had become the party's top economics adviser but had developed serious doubts over Ceauşescu's policies. In 1977 he lost all his positions, including that of professor at Bucharest University. Reduced to the rank of researcher, he refused to be silenced, hoping that through his example the status of the dissident intellectual might be regularised 'so that he may live, work and travel in dignity, tolerated, if not wholly accepted, by the authorities'.

In 1979 Radio Free Europe had broadcast a penetrating critique of Ceauşescu's economic strategy. Mihai Botez was the acknowledged author. Taking pains to appear as non-confrontational as possible, he avoided a general attack on the regime, concentrating instead on specific blunders, including the Danube canal. The evening after the broadcast Mihai, Mariana and eighteen others who had clubbed together to buy tickets were due to attend the first of a series of concerts in Bucharest. Arriving at Athéné Hall, the Botezes made their way to their seats to find that not one of their friends had turned up. They sat alone in two empty rows. That night they went on foot to each of their friends' apartments, dropping notes through the letter boxes. Nobody was to worry, they wrote: neither of them would be going to any more concerts in the series. The Botezes were never again received in their once wide circle. Mariana was demoted to a lowly position in her architectural practice, while Mihai was banished from the university altogether. By June 1987 his situation had deteriorated further.

He was twice physically attacked in the street at night by unidentified men in plain clothes. It was then that he first contemplated emigration.

Mariana's plain kitchen looked to have been untouched since the 1930s. Over a cup of herb tea, I went straight to the point, explaining to her the concept of an underground university. She surprised me by responding calmly and immediately that she believed herself to be the person to act as the focal point for our network. She emphasised what we would be letting ourselves in for and warned – as much, it seemed, for herself as for me – of the slowness of the journey and the pain it would entail. Visitors should only make contact with one Romanian at a time. It would be folly, and anyway impossible, to attempt seminars as in Czechoslovakia. She could provide an example from that very morning – an artist friend of hers who had been telephoned by an Australian who was briefly visiting Bucharest, but had been too scared even to return the call.

It seemed almost too good to be true that at my first effort I had stumbled across the key figure I was looking for. Privately I wondered how Mariana would be able to meet foreigners without incurring reprisals. Perhaps, like Pavel Bratinka, she was effectively protected by family connections – her brother Sergiu had for years been Ceauşescu's interpreter and was later to be Romania's ambassador in London. (After the dictator's execution, Sergiu Celac had his own image removed from all photographs where they appeared together.) We agreed to meet again on my return from my pilgrimage to Professor Noica, who lived in the northern mountain village of Păltiniş.

I awoke at 3.30 am from a fitful night and started at once for the town of Sibiu in my hired car, a grey Dacia, the Romanian version of a small Renault. It had proved impossible to buy a map, but Mariana had given me instructions. The first hour of the journey I wasted looking for the main road out of Bucharest. The street lighting was permanently switched off, except on the routes travelled by Ceauşescu, but even if I could have seen anything there were no road signs.

Long before dawn the car headlights picked out queues forming in front of empty bread shops, perhaps awaiting deliveries. On the rare occasion when a street name appeared, I had to get out of the car to read it. Even at this early hour there were masses of people going to work, but when I asked in my incomprehensible Romanian the way to Piteşti, the response was always apprehensive and unhelpful. At last one woman, plucking up the courage to speak to a foreigner, pointed me in the right direction. As the road deteriorated into deep ruts past Piteşti, I was thwarted by a series of slowly-moving carts, some drawn by oxen, some by horses. I braked repeatedly, on the brink of collision, alerted almost too late by the tiny lantern-jar on a stick that each cart carried at the back. At 8.30 I arrived in Sibiu. From there I took the track to Păltiniş, driving through the village of Răşinari, where each house on the cobbled main street was painted a beautiful pale yellow or green.

Noica was a marked man and I made no attempt to disguise my visit. His house, however, was hard to find. A friendly villager offered to lead me on foot through a wood up a steep mountain path strewn with pine needles. After twenty minutes' walking we reached a plateau, where my guide quietly disappeared. Ahead of me stood a hut made out of trees hewn in long flat slices. I knocked on a red painted door at the front. Noica appeared above me on a balcony, dressed in a faded green quilted jacket and brown leather spats. With nothing more than a mildly surprised look, he came down the rough flight of stairs, showing no sign of his age, and invited me up into a small room which served as his library, bedroom, washroom and workroom. In one corner stood a tall ceramic stove.

I knew the bare bones of his life story already. Having taught in Bucharest before the Communist takeover, he was exiled to a provincial town and later, ostensibly on account of a book on Goethe, charged with 'plotting against the social order' and sentenced to imprisonment and the seizure of his assets. After three years in gaol he was adopted by Amnesty as a Prisoner of Conscience, but it was a further three years before he was released. He accepted persecution as his lot and never sought the international recognition which emigration might have brought him, as it had brought his friends and contemporaries Mircea Eliade and Eugene Ionesco.

Noica's room had neither desk nor bookshelves – he did his writing on a wooden tray. On the floor and on the bed piles of letters, journals and reference books were arranged in orderly lines. At first he teased me that I had been sent as a spy, but then he was serious. Out of a striped shopping bag made of meshed plastic he methodically unloaded his life's work, about fourteen books. He commented on each one in turn. The book for which he had been arrested, *A Study of Goethe*, was incomplete, the missing part of the text having been destroyed by the Securitate. It was a measure of his isolation that he wished to tell me every detail.

We spoke in French, occasionally breaking into German when either of us was stuck. It was not hard to understand why the younger generation so venerated him. On his rare excursions to Bucharest he always drew a crowd of disciples, on whom he impressed the life or death importance of retaining, at no matter what cost, the links which bound their country to European civilisation. Had he spent his life in exile, he used to tell them, he could never have written *The Romanian Sense of Self*. This was his most profound work, in which he set out to rescue Romania from the lethal influence of Newspeak.

After a while we went to a house further up the hill, whose occupant served Noica a daily meal. As we swallowed a watery vegetable soup, I told him why I had come so far to see him. I needed his personal stamp of approval for my proposals. He listened attentively to what I had to say, nodding appreciatively and looking me directly in the eye. When I returned to Bucharest, he told me, I must make contact with his trusted pupils, Andrei Pleşu and Gabriel Liiceanu. These two, above all, would help mould my plans. When the time was right one of his followers would emerge to unite the fragmented and fearful society in which they were trapped. Meanwhile, his own task was to give meaning to the life of the philosopher, offering an example of man's ability to attain inner peace when the external conditions seemed beyond redemption.

Next day, in my hotel restaurant in Bucharest, Andrei Pleşu told me about himself. He had a comfortable shape and an air of serenity, and a pointed black beard which he stroked in a strangely reassuring way. Casually he mocked the bugging equipment concealed in the vase of flowers which had been thoughtfully placed in front of us as we sat down: 'They would have an explosive time with our conversation, but they have so many to monitor ...'

As a very young man, Andrei had come across an article in a philosophical journal. He had not previously heard of the writer, Professor Noica, who argued that Romanian words had lost their meaning and that the rediscovery of truth must begin with the reinstatement of the integrity of language. To Andrei, born into Romania's dark age, 'it was as if a bell had sounded in my mind – something that I had not felt or heard before awakened in me'. He set out to search for Noica and found his life transformed.

During the 1970s, as an up-and-coming historian in the Academy of Fine Art, he had kept his head down. Then an unpleasant incident occurred. There was at the time a craze for transcendental meditation. Two Belgian 'spiritual teachers' flew into Bucharest to supply personal mantras and give instruction in meditation to a group of initiates, including Andrei. For eighteen months all was well, until out of the blue the authorities decided that meditation was probably a cover for an insurrectionist plot. The Securitate began to follow and harass Andrei. Although he was allowed to remain in the Academy, his career as a historian was over.

He welcomed my suggestion of regular contact with British intellectuals and assured me that Gabriel Liiceanu would be of the same mind. Both of them, he told me, pursued philosophy in private. He would gladly write a piece about Romanian life for publication in Britain and looked forward to receiving any recent American or British articles on philosophical subjects, especially ethics or politics. A look of undisguised pleasure crossed his face as I gave him a copy of Kolakowski's *Totalitarianism and the Lie* – a book, so far known to him only by repute, which analysed Marxist society with devastating accuracy.

Before we finished there was something he wanted to impress on me. Material hardship mattered little to him. His family had braced themselves for the next period of starvation, the absence of heat and light, the freezing conditions of the coming winter. But what he found unbearable was the desecration of Romania. He told me:

> They are trying to kill our memories, to eliminate our history. Rather than emigrate I will remain in my country. I am at peace with this decision, but it is hard not to feel bitter. The church where my family have worshipped for generations has gone. The places where we used to meet have gone. Today there is no visible sign that the Mihai Vodă Monastery, which was founded by Prince Michael the Brave in the sixteenth century, ever existed. There is no tangible reminder of the Cantacuzino family, one of whom printed the first Romanian translation of the Bible – their tombs have been destroyed. All our past is being obliterated. Step by step Ceauşescu is ordering the annihilation of our ancient monuments. I ask myself how I can save my country from further destruction. When you go back to England, please help us.

I had no choice but to respond to his cry from the heart. Together we left the hotel and walked towards the south west part of the city, passing the formal, late nineteenth-century buildings in Calea Victoriei. Soon we turned off into the side streets. He led me to Strada Ştirbei Vodă to look at the broken remains of a church, then down Strada Bradului, where I saw for the first and last time the Bradu Staicu Church. Within days of my departure both this and the Sfânta Trâime Church would be reduced to rubble. Then we went on to see the gaping holes where once had stood the Olteni and Cuibul Barză Churches and the beautiful Sfântu Spiridon.

As we walked down empty, dirty, grey streets with refuse piled high in corners and stark shop windows displaying a single tin of food, a stick of furniture or a hideous nylon dress, I could just discern the remains of a dazzling mosaic of the architecture of pre-war Bucharest. Low-roofed houses stood in little courtyard gardens wrapped in wisteria and vine, with chickens scratching among tall eucalyptus trees and flowerbeds. Neo-classical *petits palais* would give way to six-teenth-century churches. Where the twentieth century intruded it was in the warm colours and undulating forms of Art Deco.

Andrei could not bring himself to take me further south to the historic centre of the city, where now an area the size of Westminster, Mayfair and Hyde Park had been levelled to make way for Ceauşescu's gigantic new Government palace and quarter-mile wide Boulevard to the Victory of Socialism. In this centuries-old quarter, Turkish, Greek, and Romanian houses had once jostled each other beside sixteenth-, seven-teenth- and eighteenth-century churches and monasteries, whose walls were decorated with frescoes or with dark, hierar-chical images of Byzantine boyars and princesses.

First to be demolished had been the Church of Alba Postăvar, built in the second half of the sixteenth century. Then four more shrines had been bulldozed, including the superb Cotroceni Monastery. As the new 'civic centre' rose from the rubble, further demolition continued round its edges, contami-nating an ever wider area. Again and again the population would wake to find that buildings had disappeared overnight. The inhabitants of a house might be given only a few hours' notice to evacuate a property which had been in the family for generations; then they would be forced to pay the bill for its obliteration.

At night I felt cut off and lonely. The city closed down after

8.30 and it was depressing to know that any call I made from my hotel bedroom would be monitored by the Securitate. (An acquaintance who had been left waiting in an unrepaired Government reception room shortly after an earthquake had been amused to see microphones hanging out of their ceiling sockets and wiring spilling out from cracks in the walls.) Looking for a distraction from the sinister atmosphere, I called the British Embassy and was pleasantly surprised to be asked to lunch next day by the ambassador, Hugh Arbuthnott.

After the poverty I had seen, the civilised table at the Embassy residence was another world – starched white linen napkins, delicate gold and white china, lace mats, finger bowls, three glasses at each place, one for mineral water and two for wine; and in constant attendance a maid and a butler, both listening intently to our every word. Two years later this elegant house would be burnt to a cinder as Securitate forces on the roof exchanged fire with troops below. As I sat through the formal meal, I had time to observe the tall, thin and very English ambassador.

Cutting short the coffee, Hugh Arbuthnott led me away from the other guests into the garden. It would be safer to talk there, although he suspected that with their newest technology the Securitate could pick up much of what we said even out of doors. 'Why are you here?' he asked. Cautiously I outlined the plans a group of us intended to put in motion when I returned to England. I had already warmed to him; there was none of the self-satisfied superiority I had sometimes encountered among our diplomats elsewhere in Eastern Europe. Even so, I was taken aback by the sympathy and enthusiasm of his response. He offered to help wherever he could and invited me to stay on my next visit – unless, he quickly added, this would be counter-productive.

Among my contacts in Bucharest there was one – a theatre director whom I will call B – who I was sure was a Securitate informer. His name had been given to me by Dennis Deletant. B's louche and dissolute appearance, his evident confidence that he was safe in meeting me and his material possessions, including high-tech electrical equipment, told me all I needed to know. It was a pleasing irony that the production he took me to one evening should be *Coriolanus*. The packed auditorium relished Shakespeare's depiction of a flawed commander, who treated the rabble of ordinary humanity with contempt – the difference from Ceaușescu being that Coriolanus recognised the need to live at a heroic level if that contempt were to be carried off, whereas Ceaușescu was a small and brutish vandal, who had done nothing to merit the powers that he assumed.

On the morning of my last full day in Bucharest I called again on Mariana Celac. She told me that with the worsening political and economic climate the Securitate was finding it increasingly difficult to rely on the information it obtained from its army of informers (said to be one in three of the population) and had switched its emphasis to bugging. The recent Western focus on human rights had also had its effect in that high profile dissidents were now generally harassed, intimidated and hauled in for interrogation, rather than imprisoned or assassinated. For the lesser known, an alternative treatment was compulsory 'medication' in provincial mental hospitals. Torture and coma-inducing drugs were applied to the inmates, who were kept in degrading conditions and often reduced to zombies. When released, few could any longer be classed as sane.

Abroad, the Securitate were as violent as ever. Romanians working for Radio Free Europe seemed particularly targeted. Within a period of ten years, three service directors, Noel Bernard, Mihai Cismărescu and Vlad Georgescu, died prematurely of cancer, perhaps victims of Operation Radu, a project to irradiate the enemies of the regime. Monica Lovinescu, a senior editor, was beaten up in Paris, 'to prevent her writing and talking', according to Ion Pacepa, former head of Ceaușescu's intelligence service. Preda Bunescu, another editor, was found dead at home under suspicious circumstances; Ion Chiriac, a disc jockey, was knifed to death; Emil Georgescu, a programme editor, recovered from an unexplained car crash, but was subsequently stabbed twenty-two times and died of his wounds; and Paul Goma and Virgil Tănase, both of whom wrote for broadcasting, received parcel bombs. Five Romanian diplomats were expelled from Germany for conspiring to blow up Radio Free Europe's Munich headquarters. Mariana Celac was worried that the Securitate's long arm might reach her departed husband in the United States. As for me, I could not help reflecting that foreigners, too, might not be immune.

Even after Ceaușescu's fall the Securitate made me nervous. Old fears were rekindled in 1990 when I criticised in print the choice of Bogdan Baltazar, Ceaușescu's former Securitate chief in the Philippines, as a Director of the EBRD, a bank formed to finance Eastern Europe's reconstruction. Word reached me that Baltazar had exploded with rage when he read the article and was out 'to kill' me. A similar message came from Ceaușescu's tame Rabbi, Moses Rosen, whose autobiography I had reviewed unfavourably in the *Spectator*.

Mariana had given much thought to our previous conversation. The ideas she came up with were imaginative. She wanted to set up meetings with the Union of Architects or, failing that, the Union of Writers. She was horrified by the devastation of Bucharest and gave me a map to pass to Mihnea Berindei in Paris marked with the most recent destructions. She had reason to believe that sixty or seventy more churches were scheduled for bulldozing and that an even larger abomination was afoot. The 'systematisation' of Bucharest, as it was officially termed the following spring, was part of a project to restructure the whole of Romania. Apartment blocks would replace individual houses and in the villages the peasant smallholders – with house, cow, pig, fruit trees and little vegetable garden – would be uprooted and herded into multi-storey agro-industrial complexes.

Mariana believed that Ceaușescu planned to dehumanise the rural population so as to make it as easily controlled and spied upon as the people in the cities. Seven thousand villages were scheduled for demolition by the end of the century. The destruction of the past was Ceauşescu's means of leaving his mark on history, of creating a brave new world of asphalt and concrete that would last for an eternity. On the grounds that finesse would be more effective than confrontation, Mariana suggested that we arrange a travelling exhibition of contrasting architectural heritages – Romanian church buildings and monuments, and English country houses and town buildings. To make the point, she asked that the British section show examples of successful preservation and restoration.

Ceauşescu had recently thought up a ghastly plan to hold a festival of anthems and national songs for amateurs, in which everyone, however unmusical, would participate. Mariana thought this might provide an opening for me to locate a willing British choral society which could be put in touch with a counterpart in Romania through the Committee for Culture. She knew, for instance, of a genuine Romanian wind orchestra for miners. On this innocuous pretext, the visitors might discover for themselves what was happening in the country and spread the word at home. Her requests for herself were modest – principally articles on architecture and design. She asked, too, if I could persuade the American Embassy to reinstate the sale of *Newsweek* and *Time*. A few copies used to be sold there, but now they had been stopped. She hoped the British Embassy might do the same for *Encounter*. She used to save up to buy these magazines.

Lastly we discussed Romania's environmental problems, which were catastrophic even by Eastern European standards. Mariana wanted me to introduce the British environmentalist Tom Burke to Ion Iliescu, whom she described as an 'interesting' man, who used to be the minister for water resources but had fallen out of favour and now ran an obscure publishing house in Bucharest called Editura Tecnică. Her idea was that Burke should write to Iliescu explaining that he had read his article on water pollution and would welcome an exchange of views. According to Mariana, Iliescu was appalled by what he had seen as a minister and was looking for ways for the facts to come out without him being fingered as the source of the story. All this in whispers, in Mariana's kitchen. Then she wrote on a scrap of paper that Iliescu was spoken of as a possible successor to Ceauşescu.

This was the first time I had come across the name of the man who would become President of Romania after Ceauşescu's overthrow. He had held a variety of posts during the dictatorship, including those of ideology chief and minister for youth. The word in émigré circles was that he had joined a Soviet-backed conspiracy to oust Ceauşescu, the three leading plotters being from the old *nomenklatura* – Nicolae Militaru, an ex-army officer dismissed for spying for the USSR, Silviu Brucan,[1] a former ambassador to Washington, and Virgil Măgureanu, a Securitate officer. Some years later, although the full truth about Iliescu's coup[2] may never be known, these guesses would be substantially confirmed. Mariana's family had some links to Iliescu (her brother, for example, became ambassador to Britain), but though my head sometimes counselled caution, my heart told me that she was on the side of the angels.

After leaving Mariana I headed for the southern part of Bucharest to look at the area around the Boulevard of the Victory of Socialism beyond the point I had reached with Andrei Pleşu. I could see why Mariana had referred to it as 'Nagasaki'. An avenue of skeletal apartment blocks with windows like empty hollow eyes petered out towards the east, leading nowhere; as I turned westward I became aware of a vast crescent of government buildings and then – suddenly – the looming, atrocious House of the Republic. Grotesquely out of

---

1 In 1984 Brucan had approached the KGB for special weapons with which to immobilise the Ceauşescu loyalists in the Politburo – guns with silencers which could shoot narcotic darts. But with Andropov on his deathbed the Kremlin was not yet ready to make its move.
2 On 22 December 1989, when Ceauşescu fled his Bucharest palace, no less than three different cliques aspired to succeed to his powers. The ultimate winner was Iliescu's NSF.

proportion to its surroundings, dwarfing any building I had ever seen – Buckingham Palace a mere town house in comparison – this gigantic edifice sickened me as I remembered Andrei Pleşu's description of what once had been.

My last vision was of the Church of Prince Michael the Brave, which two years before had stood directly in the path of Ceauşescu's triumphal vista. Offensive to the eye of the dictator, the monastic settlement which surrounded it had been bulldozed and the church itself hoisted on wooden rollers and placed naked and alone in the imperial socialist wilderness, 300 yards from its original position.

Wandering listlessly through this unpopulated desert, I eventually found at its periphery, blocked by ripped-up trees lying wounded on their sides, the pretty little street called Strada Parfumului where Sylvia Kerim lived, a designer of children's books. Grateful to be back among buildings on a human scale, I pushed open an iron gate and peered into the garden before knocking on the door of Sylvia's house, which was charmingly decorated with Islamic detail. She was in a highly nervous state, reduced to incoherence by the noise of the lorries and cement-mixers and the clouds of dust and rubble. She prayed that her luck would hold: close as the bulldozers had come, she had not yet received notice of evacuation.

In my hotel I fell into a deep sleep. I was due to catch an early flight next day. Late that night the telephone rang. As if in a Graham Greene novel, I heard a voice, evidently from the foyer, saying: 'McGuinness here. British Embassy. On duty. Could we meet? Outside the hotel, in the street?' Shuffling into some clothes I walked down four flights to the empty reception area, out through the glass doors and into the darkness. The name was unfamiliar to me and so far as I was concerned anything could have been afoot. But McGuinness proved genuine. We circled the hotel several times while he gave me a message from the ambassador. Before checking in at the airport, would I please hand over my notes and destroy all my Romanian addresses? Would I also please give him any documents that I had received during my visit? They would reach me in London by Thursday morning through the diplomatic bag.

I was impressed. Hugh Arbuthnott was not to know that my notes and addresses were in code and that I was well aware that the Securitate could trace the author of any typescript through the typeface.[3] The offer of the diplomatic bag, which I had sought in vain in Czechoslovakia, was of great potential value. But I could not help wondering if there was an element of self-interest in this unexpected generosity. By late 1987 Foreign Office policy was shifting. London might well have been looking for a more detailed impression of the dissident community. A list of my contacts would have done wonders for the Embassy's reputation in Whitehall.

As we rounded the block for the third time, McGuinness turned the conversation to other matters. He told me how devastated he was to be leaving Romania in two weeks' time. After three years, neither he nor his wife would ever be the same again. He poured out his anxiety at having to hold in his head so many official lies and so much suffering – with nothing written down for fear of compromising his Romanian friends. What was he to do? I told him he must write a book on his return to give voice to the Romanian tragedy. My diary that evening noted the intense sadness his account had stirred in me.

---

3 Since 1983 the renting or lending of a typewriter was forbidden by decree of the State Council. Private owners had to have authorisation from the militia, which could be issued only after a written request containing details of the type and design number of the typewriter; how it was obtained (purchase, gift, inheritance); and for what purpose it was to be used. If the authorisation was granted, the applicant had to report with the machine at the militia office to provide a typing specimen. A similar specimen had to be provided during the first two months of each year, as well as after every repair. If the authorisation was refused the typewriter had to be sold within ten days (evidenced by a bill of sale) or given to an authorised person. Anyone inheriting a typewriter or receiving one as a gift had to apply for immediate authorisation. Defective typewriters which could no longer be repaired had to be sent to a collecting-point and surrendered to the militia.

Perhaps I, too, would never be quite the same again. Romania's fate was poignant beyond my ability to express it. I was haunted by Andrei Pleşu's words: 'Step by step they are destroying our memories. Step by step all details of the past are being eliminated ...'

Fifteen

Christine Stone, a lawyer and journalist, who was married to the historian Norman Stone, had spent much of her honeymoon in Romania in 1979 and had formed an affection for the country. Together we decided to set up a trust, which we named after the nineteenth-century poet Mihai Eminescu. We soon found a nucleus of trustees. Christine introduced Mark Almond, a young history don at Oxford with an encyclopedic knowledge of the Soviet empire and an irresistibly wry method of expressing himself. For my part, I approached the Hobbes scholar, historian and fluent Romanian speaker Noel Malcolm, who had recently left Cambridge for a spell as a journalist on the *Spectator*. Later we added Miranda Villiers, who had spent many years in Romania when her husband was cultural attaché there, and John Laughland, a polymath at the Sorbonne with a Romanian mother.

We selected our patrons with equal care. The response to our invitations was encouraging. The eminent Byzantine historian Steven Runciman wrote that he still had friends in Romania from the pre-war days and felt strongly that practical support was needed 'if any cultural life is to survive the present monstrous regime'. The writer and traveller Paddy Leigh Fermor was equally positive:

The Mihai Eminescu (excellent poet!) Trust is a very good idea and should do a lot of good. The last time I went there, 3 years ago, the situation was beastly – ill-lit towns, nothing to eat, and fear. I hired a car with Rumanian number plates so gave lifts to about 15 peasants and workmen a day (over a week revisiting old haunts, mostly in Transylvania). If I gave

[147]

a lift to a couple, they murmured half-hearted and insincere praise of the status quo, terrified of detection; but each <u>solitary</u> pick-up poured out a stream of misery and hate. It was harrowing.

Six more patrons completed the list: Yehudi Menuhin, who in his youth had been taught by the Romanian composer Georges Enescu; the historian Professor Hugh Trevor-Roper, who had an important dissident link among Romanian academics; Lionel Bloch, a Romanian émigré solicitor; Sherban Cantacuzino, head of the Royal Fine Arts Commission, who had been educated in England in the 1950s and had never returned to Romania; the Oxford medievalist Professor Demetri Obolensky; George Urban, the Soviet analyst and head of Radio Free Europe; and the MP George Walden.

Our main objective was to alter received opinion about Romania. Despite everything, Ceauşescu's image as an enlightened socialist was still generally accepted in the Anglo-Saxon world. This reputation had been dented by some savage exposés, notably by Bernard Levin in *The Times*, but Romania had nevertheless been upgraded to normal trading terms (known misleadingly as MFN, or Most Favored Nation status) by the United States, while in the past Presidents Nixon and Ford had boosted the dictator's stock by visiting Bucharest. We set ourselves the specific targets that Ceauşescu should not receive a visit from President Reagan or have Romania's MFN status renewed. At the same time we kept our eyes open for academics with the journalistic touch and enough hardiness to brave Romanian conditions.

I took Mariana Celac's advice and concentrated on Romania's history and culture, writing to *The Times* and the *New York Times* to report how many historic buildings had been destroyed and how much more destruction was to follow:

I have a map showing new areas scheduled for demolition...the patriarchal Cathedral of the Romanian Orthodox Church and sixty or seventy other churches have a few weeks' respite before the bulldozers start to move in. Representations to UNESCO have proved useless, for UNESCO is no longer a neutral body and does its best to deflect any criticism of the Communist powers. It therefore rests on the British Government, the European Community and the United States to exert whatever pressure they can ...

The letter attracted attention and I was commissioned to write a story for the *Daily Mail*. This never saw the light of day. It was scheduled to go to print on the night of the great windstorm which swept southern England in October 1987, coinciding with the heaviest stock market crash since 1929, and the features editor decided that his readers would have more pressing concerns on their minds than the rape of Romania. A few days later, however, I placed the article in an American paper and it was syndicated around the United States. In England I gave a more comprehensive version to the Keston College Journal, *Frontier*, whose editor asked me to find some distinguished co-signatories. The first person I approached, knowing that as an architect he would be receptive, was the Duke of Gloucester. Under the heading 'Architectural Vandalism' he added a contribution of his own, drawing attention to the international Charter on Historic Towns, which Romania had recently ratified and which was drawn up specifically to preserve what Ceauşescu was destroying.

The Duke's intervention had the desired effect. It became a news story in its own right, as well as drawing in the support of the architectural establishment. My letter to *The Times* also gave us a useful lead, when a young independent filmmaker, Julian Woropay, wrote that he wanted to record Ceauşescu's destruction on film. Fresh out of art school, he asked whether I could suggest any sources of information and finance. Until then the Mihai Eminescu Trust had only given money for books; Julian Woropay became our first exception.

Lone voices count for little and our articles, letters and meetings with politicians were but small drips competing against a sea of 'reputable' information. At the end of 1987, however, the publication of two books from political insiders was to have a far-reaching influence on Western opinion-makers. The first, *Pinstripes and Reds*, by the former US ambassador to Romania, David Funderburk, described the refusal of officials in the US State Department to accept the testimony of their own staff on the ground describing Romania. Ceauşescu was playing a double game, exploiting Romania's trading status to obtain banned technological exports for the Soviet Union. While the Soviets connived at the projection of harmless political differences, Nixon was writing to Ceauşescu on the dictator's sixty-fifth birthday to tell him he was 'one of the greatest leaders of the world, who valiantly carries out an independent foreign policy'.

Funderburk's revelations paled alongside those of Ceauşescu's Chief of Intelligence, Ion Pacepa, who had defected to America in 1978 and remains in hiding to this day. His *Red Horizons,* written in racy style and exuding authenticity, was crammed with disgusting anecdotes of Ceauşescu's private life. Pacepa's descriptions of sinister plans to deceive the West, of carcinogenic rays beamed into the cells of political prisoners and of the sadistic antics of Ceauşescu's son Nicu came as a vivid confirmation of all the stories we had heard. Ceauşescu had panicked when he heard that the book was to be serialised by Radio Free Europe. Summoning the American ambassador, Roger Kirk, he demanded that the transmission be cancelled. Nothing could make Ceauşescu grasp that the radio station was not a government agency, a prejudice shared by many Western liberals, who spoke of it contemptuously as a CIA front. In fact it operated under the guidance of an independent board. The members were appointed by the US President, but their mission was to provide uncensored news. For our dissident contacts behind the Iron Curtain Radio Free Europe ranked with the BBC World Service as their two principal sources of reliable information.

In November, in an emergency attempt to keep industry supplied with energy, Ceauşescu ordered thirty percent cuts in gas and electricity for domestic consumption. Word had it that in the cities people could be without electricity for much of the day and that gas pressure would be so restricted that it would only be possible to cook after midnight. Mariana Celac's elderly mother never left the house. At least she could cook when the power came on, assuming she had any ingredients worth cooking. In the back gardens of the village, something of a market economy still operated. In the summer months peasants grew vegetables and fruit, in the autumn they stored, pickled or dried much of their harvest. Ordinarily, produce was brought into the towns once a week; but deliveries could not now be guaranteed and for the first time an influx of peasants had appeared in Bucharest not selling, but searching for food. I had images of poor Noica with a tiny electric heater at his house in Păltiniş, reduced to an hour's warmth a day. At the end of the year, he died. I wrote his obituary for *The Times*.

It was not easy to tempt an academic to go to Bucharest but we found a willing one at last in David Selbourne, who after criticising the fundamental faith of the Labour Party in 1985, had been prevented by pickets from teaching politics at Ruskin College, Oxford. While preparing his court case for unfair dismissal, he had time for travel and journalism. Before his departure, we briefed him carefully: never to telephone people, never to give the name of one contact to another, never to take a taxi and never to go direct to a destination.

Returning chilled by his experiences, Selbourne submitted an extended piece for the *Sunday Telegraph*. The editor's title for the two-page spread – 'Visions of a Marxist Hell' – was melodramatic, but the economic situation had deteriorated far beyond what I had seen in the summer. Selbourne described filthy remnants of food in the empty shops, no meat, butter rationed to a matchbox quantity once a month, bread rationed but still virtually unobtainable. There was a chilling description of a meat queue:

For sale is a consignment – contained in large cartons being broken open by assistants as the crowd presses in on them – of frozen chicken heads and necks, feet and wings; the torsos are most likely to be in the Soviet Union under a meat-for-oil barter, which every year takes thousands of tonnes of Romanian meat to Moscow…Out of each box comes an impacted jellied mass, some three feet square, of broken up chicken pieces; you can see blue eyes staring bleakly from these icebergs, white scraggy wings, black-spiked, as if with splinters, and a tumble of feet, yellow talons, curled and stiffened. At noon, when I passed again, the queue was longer, the press as intense as ever. By then the congealed chicken-blocks had begun to melt into a bloody flux of half-frozen meat; it was being manhandled, with purple fingers, from sodden cardboard into plastic bags, juices dripping.

Selbourne confirmed that the Bucharest intellectuals wanted us to visit them as frequently as possible – I had been worried that their real wishes might be concealed by their manners. In his report he wrote:

In the next phase the politically experienced and those with knowledge of other Eastern European countries will be most appreciated. Building up contacts in Romania is relatively more important for the free-thinking intellectuals than anywhere else in E. Europe. They are far more isolated, but in this volatile period in Romanian affairs the effect will be disproportionately large. And though dissidents are generally too suspicious to meet each other face to face, especially if a foreigner is present, I am assured that each person has access to others who are eager for material we can get to any one individual.

Andrei Pleşu had finished his article on 'the philosophical life' in Romania, and hoped it would be collected by the next visitor. He could not post it, since his typewriter had been registered. He wanted Béla Basó, from the University of Budapest, to invite him to give a paper on Goethe's theory of colours. A formal invitation would give him a good chance of getting a visa and the visit would help develop contacts between Hungary and Romania.

The journals we had sent Pleşu through the post had arrived but he was not sure if Noica's had reached him. Pleşu had 'about thirty friends' to whom he would circulate the reading matter we provided. Three of these had already seen the quarterly journal on Soviet Affairs, *Survey;* they would also like the *London Review of Books* and the *New York Review of Books.* We must be sure to post them with their wrappers stamped with the name of an academic institution; it was dangerous to receive materials despatched privately. We should not send individual books on philosophy, but could safely send the complete series of *Oxford Readings in Philosophy* to the Director of the Institute of Fine Arts.

Mariana Celac told Selbourne that she had passed round the journals and books I had left with her in September and was still thinking of other people with whom we might be in direct contact. She reiterated her interest in articles on architecture which might help her work on urban decay. When Selbourne told her of the Church report, *Faith in the Inner City,* she asked whether we could get one of its authors to make an official visit to Bucharest. And could she have material on the restoration of old buildings and their integration into modern life – for instance, the renewal of the docks areas in London and Liverpool?

Mariana had a remarkably detailed knowledge of British cultural institutions and suggested that we try to interest the Civic Trust and the RIBA in the Romanian plight. She brightened when Selbourne told her that we had approached the Royal Fine Arts Commission with her idea of a touring architectural exhibition. This project caused a minor crisis in our ranks when I suggested that the Charles Douglas-Home Trust, set up in Charlie's memory, should contribute £5,000, only to be vetoed by one trustee on the grounds that I should not involve the trust in my 'anti-Communist activities'. I was very hurt at the time. There were few ideas which would have so appealed to Charlie and I was mortified at having to tell Mariana that the exhibition had to be deferred. In the event, it did not take place until after the 1989 revolution.

When Selbourne met the contact I have referred to as B, he formed the same view as I had. 'I did not like him! I felt him to be shady, or a bit cracked, or both; this may be unfair. But he is not, it seems to me, terribly reliable. He has a powerful position in the theatre, is a well-known public figure and is pretty cynical.'

Determined to see more of Romania than its capital, Selbourne set off north to Cluj in Transylvania for the last part of his visit, in search of Doina Cornea, who had taught French literature at Cluj University for over twenty years. In the summer of 1982 she had smuggled out to the West an open letter describing the spiritual draining of the Romanian people by the regime, 'a people without a scale of moral values ... a people fed solely on slogans'. In her last paragraph she apologised for not revealing her name; she considered it more important to be able to continue teaching her students. Unfortunately, owing to a misunderstanding (she had signed the letter to demonstrate its authenticity), when Radio Free Europe broadcast the text it named Cornea as the signatory.

The authorities took some time to destroy her career. Interrogated by the Securitate, then denounced in a meeting of teaching staff at the university, Cornea was pensioned off a year after the broadcast, dismissed by the rector for 'inciting the youth to disobedience' on the grounds that she had given her students a prominent émigré's diary to read and had suggested in class that Romanian culture was being discredited by the compromise of intellectuals.

Cornea continued writing open letters to Ceauşescu and for the first time since Goma it seemed that someone had appeared with the courage to state the truth in a loud, clear voice. We were determined to give her all the help she needed, but Selbourne's attempt to call on her was blocked by police in her street, posted at the junction with the main road. His report identified Cluj as a promising, if difficult, territory: 'How immensely worthwhile it would be to make more contacts in this city, full of academics and students, very tense... I felt frustrated at not having real access, especially to Hungarians. It is out of the question to phone anyone in Cluj.'

A week after Selbourne's return food riots broke out across Romania, the worst uprising being on 15 November 1987 in the industrial centre of Braşov. The mood became particularly angry after 25,000 workers from a truck factory went unpaid and 22,000 in the Steagul Rosa plant had their wages cut – this blow falling on the day of the local elections, in which voting was compulsory. A large crowd gathered in the central square, tore down the sign of the Braşov Party headquarters and smashed the windows to bring out sackfuls of cheese, margarine and bread for the starving populace. From a nearby rooftop the Securitate videoed the demonstration. For two or three days after the riots the Government isolated the city, forbidding trains to stop at Braşov and requiring special permits for drivers wishing to enter the centre. Eventually 400 arrests were made. Some 60 were brought to Bucharest, tried and sentenced to prison for 'hooliganism'.

News of the riots on the BBC spurred Doina Cornea to further heroism. Later that night she and her son prepared leaflets calling on other workers to express support for the Braşov victims. Together they distributed them outside several Cluj factories. But their sacrificial protest found no echo among the local inhabitants. From Raţiu's *Free Romania* we learned that both of them were arrested and imprisoned the following day.

More surprisingly, public criticism of the Braşov incident came from a high-ranking individual in the Romanian *nomenklatura*, Silviu Brucan. As one of the few surviving members of the early Romanian Communist Party, he had been deputy chief editor of the Party newspaper, *Scânteia*, from 1944 to 1956. A ruthless ideologue, he had at that time encouraged the herding of the peasant population into collective farms and had called for the death penalty for those who opposed the Communist takeover. He went on to become Romania's ambassador to the United Nations.

In recent years, despite lacking a university diploma, Brucan had been professor of Marxism at Bucharest University. No longer part of Ceauşescu's inner circle, he had turned cautiously non-conformist. His willingness to expound the 'flaws' in contemporary Communism caused ripples of excitement among Bucharest's foreign diplomats. This was, however, an exaggerated response to Brucan's articles. Romanians with good Moscow links could speak against the regime without much harm coming to them, provided they were in tune with Soviet orthodoxy and avoided direct attacks on Ceauşescu. Brucan's comments on Braşov were pure Gorbachev.

> A watershed in Romania's political history as a socialist state has been reached [he wrote]. A period of crisis has opened up in the relationship between the Communist Party and the working class ...The leadership is now facing a hard choice: mass repression, because we are dealing with thousands of workers, or a sincere effort to come to terms with their legitimate grievances. Certainly the prevailing trend ... speaks loudly in favour of the second option. Repression may only result in total isolation, this time not only from the West but from the East.

For a short while after his criticism, Brucan's access to foreigners was curtailed. But after a brief spell of house arrest the authorities eased off and by next year he was again able to travel abroad and join the Embassy dining round. When I met him in 1990, what I saw was a rotund, elderly, calculating and superficially urbane man, now a member of the ruling neo-Communist National Salvation Front Party and chairman of its foreign policy commission. He took great delight in showing photographs taken by the Securitate of himself entering the American Embassy. These had been mysteriously extracted from his dossier after the revolution.

During a three-day visit to Bucharest four months before the Braşov crisis, Gorbachev had made it clear that he was displeased by several aspects of Romania's economic and social policies. There were signs that Ceauşescu was shaken. He postponed the annual National Party Conference and sent a substitute to Gorbachev's briefing for Warsaw Pact leaders in East Berlin. Then out of the blue he granted an amnesty to a large number of prisoners – not political dissidents but convicted offenders, whose release into society caused real alarm.

By January 1988 even Russian journalists felt free to describe the miseries of Romania. A reporter from *Komsomolskaya Pravda* descibed how he froze in a flat in Bucharest that had no warm water and almost no lighting. Other Russian journalists followed suit. In the end Ceauşescu's human rights record became too grotesque for the United States to renew Romania's MFN status. To forestall the humiliation of exclusion, Ceauşescu renounced MFN unilaterally. Now all Romanian products arriving in American ports would be subject to higher duties.

During the coldest part of the year, in February, Mark Almond felt it was his turn to go to Bucharest. He had been given the address of Andrei Pippidi, the grandson and son of two well-known historians. Pippidi had taken up a short scholarship in Oxford in the seventies but had been prevented from returning to take his PhD. He had signed a letter of protest to Ceauşescu on the destruction of historic monuments. He spoke beautiful English and once Mark had met him he became one of our leading Romanian links.

Mark's first attempt at a meal in Romania was memorable. The waiter in the Chinese restaurant in Strada Anca Ipatescu, where Pippidi lived, took their order but returned after forty-five minutes to say that the gas was too low to cook the meat.

Another night, after tramping the streets in search of Andrei Pleşu, Mark returned to his hotel to find the place in darkness. Having had no food all day, he asked at the desk for some sort of nourishment. The receptionist took him to the back kitchen, a vast room which was meant to provide food for the hotel, and opened the door of the industrial fridge. It was empty except for one strange-looking chop. A lone figure in the kitchen agreed to fry it for him, but after an hour the pale light from a flicker of gas again failed to produce enough heat to complete its cooking.

On his return, Mark tried his hand at journalism.

I sent various versions of an article to everywhere from the *Spectator* to the *Daily Mail*, but I have had no luck. Christine [Stone] gave a set of my photographs to a man from *World in Action*. Perhaps they might end up doing a programme – although in Granada's hands it will probably turn out as a paean to Ceauşescu's public housing just as Thatcher is cutting the Welfare State, etc, etc.

He did, however, add to the *Times* correspondence column.

… It seems that the Romanian Government is abiding by its promise not to destroy any more churches. However, even though churches in the path of the redevelopment are being shunted aside on vast steel contraptions, all the non-sacred buildings associated with such a church still fall prey to the bulldozers – along with all the homes, shops, and trees in the parish.

One of our more subversive schemes needed cooperation from the National Gallery. We wanted to find a way to get a photocopier to Andrei Pleşu and Mariana Celac. Neil Mac-Gregor, Director of the National Gallery, agreed to act as a 'front', provided that his Board did not object and that we paid the bill. In February 1988 he was able to give me the news that his trustees had agreed to present a photocopier to the Institute of Fine Art in Bucharest. He enclosed a formal letter to the Institute, which we had drafted for him in our best Newspeak.

12th February 1988

Dear Mr Gheorghiu,

The Trustees of the National Gallery have recently been considering relations between fine art institutions in Western and Eastern Europe. We have decided upon certain proposals which we hope will develop academic relations amongst all European countries. Our aim is to further the mutual intellectual concerns of our joint cultural heritage. In order to facilitate communications between us and as a gesture of goodwill, we would like to offer the Institute of Fine Art in Bucharest a photocopier. We hope this machine, although rather small, would suit your requirements.

It would be necessary to go to Romania as soon as possible to check out with Andrei and Mariana where to install this innocent-sounding piece of potential dynamite so that they could have ready access to it. In the meanwhile, however, fascinating events were happening in Czechoslovakia. I was tempted to make a quick visit to hear how Bratinka saw the situation there.

Although Miloş Jakeş, the new Czech Communist Party leader, was talking cautiously about the need for *perestroika* along Soviet lines, there had been little let up in the harassment of human rights activists. On 7 March, 10,000 people had responded to Cardinal Tomášek's call to attend a mass at St Vitus's Cathedral in the grounds of Prague Castle, in honour of the blessed Agnes of Bohemia (a thirteenth-century princess who had renounced her title to found a hospice). A large crowd had gathered outside Tomášek's palace, chanting demands for religious freedom and pleading for a visit from the Pope. Arrayed in purple and gold vestments, Tomášek appeared on the balcony to great applause and spoke to the demonstrators: 'Christ is our strength and will also be our victory.' The secret police mingled with the crowd without intervening, but later that evening a familiar spoiling operation went into action. Bratinka, Benda, Havel and twenty other prominent dissidents were detained, while others were turned back in the street outside the home of a British diplomat where they had been invited to dine.

Bratinka, in high spirits and with his usual prescience, passed a message to me: 'Please come if you can. The Brezhnev doctrine is dead. The Soviet machine will no longer have the will to resort to military intervention if dissent gets out of control in Eastern Europe.' I would have liked to feel the atmosphere for myself. But for the moment Romania had to be the priority.

Author and her husband Charles Douglas-Home at home at Knights Mill
a year before he died. Author's painting.

Early yesterday morning Charles Douglas-Home, our Defence Correspondent, was ordered out of Czechoslovakia. Eighteen hours earlier he was detained at gun point by a Russian Army unit. Here is the story of his arrest and lengthy interrogation by the Russians and Czechs before final expulsion.

I was expelled from Czechoslovakia at 4.15 a.m. yesterday, when three secret police escorted me to the frontier post at Bratislava. The formal expulsion order was actually served on me shortly before midnight at the Tatry police headquarters at Banska Bystrica, a spa in the Tatry mountains about 120 miles from Bratislava, but by then I had already been under arrest for 14 hours—three of which had been spent in Russian hands, and eight taken up with interrogations by a collection of Czechoslovak security officials.

I was first arrested at 10 a.m. on Thursday when I was seized by Russian officers and men of an armoured unit and dragged from my car. This operation was made more complicated because the Russians, in their eagerness to lay hands on me, forgot to undo my safety harness. Thus they mistook the resistance provided by this harness to be my own resistance, and interrupted their efforts to me.

I was in no mood to resist them, faced as I was by the muzzles of several sentries' sub-machine guns.

The incident took place on a minor road near the town of Zilina, in Slovakia, where a Russian armoured column was stationed. The column was split up into four parts and consisted of about 500 vehicles, including tanks and armoured cars. I had discovered the column on the previous Monday after driving round most of Slovakia looking for Russian units which were making such a slow withdrawal from the country.

The armoured column parked near Zilina was making a mockery of the announcements from Prague about Russian troops, not only because of its size but also because of the claims that only a few small units were left—the column must have numbered at least 2,000 men in fighting units—but also because its immobility contradicted the impression generated by Prague that the columns were all on the move.

Having drawn a blank at Sliac I returned to Zilina, carrying out my usual check on the tank unit on the way. Unknown to me, at the instigation of the Russians, the Czech police had erected a "no entry" sign on the bridle road leading down past the column. They had done this because the Russians had complained about the attentions of the many cars driving past, including my beige Volkswagen with the Austrian number plate.

I was not actually stopped by the Soviet guards at the beginning of the bridle road when I turned in off the main road, and was allowed to cruise down the hill until I came opposite the main tank park, when armed guards with fixed bayonets and supported by several officers strode out from the ditch and barred my path.

An officer climbed into my car and ordered me to get out. I asked to see the Czechoslovak police, which appeared to anger him, and at this point his men started to lay hands on me and eventually succeeded in dragging me from the car. They then half pushed and half lifted the car—its steering had been locked when I removed the key—into the camp area.

I was hustled and bustled off the road—still protesting that I wished to see the Czech police—and ordered to crawl into a low, small tent at the gateway to the camp. I was not keen to ...

often deliberately obtuse, but it had a definite theme—what extra interest in the Soviet military forces did I have, apart from my journalistic one? They were once again trying, by implication, to accuse me of spying.

There were occasional diversionary exercises, such as when it was suggested that I was liable to a year's imprisonment for reporting details about the Soviet strengths, when I was asked to show my notebooks to see if they corroborated what I had claimed that I reported all that I saw; when I was asked what particular special training I had received before coming on a job like this.

In answering, I tried to stick to the one important point. If there were charges pending, could they please name the possible charge against me. If there were not, would they say so.

Of course there were no charges, of course nothing I said could be used against me. Then what was the point of any further questions ...

9 p.m., when the police chief again left the room. He came back to say that my car number had been incorrectly entered on my visa, although this had been done by the customs officials themselves.

I thought this was the start of a new tack, but then he departed again for a telephone call and finally returned to say that my presence in Czechoslovakia was no longer considered desirable to the Ministry of the Interior in Prague, and that I was to be expelled. We were to go to Banska Bystrica to collect the formal expulsion order and then I would drive under escort, through the night to Bratislava. I had not been allowed to telephone my hotel all day, nor was I initially allowed to telephone colleagues in Prague to tell them what had happened.

The police chief ultimately agreed to one call to Prague while I was packing at the hotel, but as I should have been able to predict by then the line to Prague ...

Douglas-Home, back in London yesterday, retraces his movements near Zilina before his arrest.

Charlie's article in *The Times* describing his arrest

Diana Phipps as 'Madame Polasky' fortune-telling
to raise money for the Czechs.

LEFT Knights Mill   RIGHT The first of the author's series of crucifixion paintings completed a year before Charlie's illness.

The author with sons Tara and Luke

Author's portrait of Roger Scruton
(his father looming in the background)

LEFT Cardinal Tomášek   RIGHT Father Popiełuszko taking a service in
St Kostka's Church. He was murdered shortly afterwards.

After Popiełuszko's murder, the Pope visited his grave near Warsaw.

LEFT Etching by the author after her first visit to Poland. RIGHT Scene from the author's journey to Sibiu in Romania.

Pavel Bratinka in the polluted forest outside Most.

LEFT Author's etching for lecture to Brno artists. RIGHT Author's portrait
of Agnieszka Kolakowska, who was expelled and ordered
never to visit Romania again.

During the building of the Boulevard to the Victory of Socialism,
churches were uprooted and shunted out of the way on rollers.

LEFT Mariana Celac outside the Romanian Orthodox Church in Snagor,
near Bucharest. RIGHT Nicu Steinhardt, who was betrayed in his
monastery and had his most secret manuscript stolen.

The Boulevard to the Victory of Socialism, leading to
Ceauşescu's half-built palace

Sixteen

After some reflection, I accepted Hugh and Vanessa Arbuth-nott's invitation to stay at the Embassy residence in Bucharest. Thinking that my letters and articles over the previous six months might prevent me from getting a visa if I applied in London in the normal way, I took the chance of arriving at Otopeni airport without one – unusually Romania operated a visa system at the point of entry.

It was a relief to find Vanessa at the barrier, thrusting forward a letter embossed with the Foreign Office crest stating that I was a guest of Her Majesty's Government. On sight of the impressive array of stamps the border officials immediately waved me through. When Hugh came home from lunch we discussed my plans in mime language and notes. I wrote down that I would like to visit dissidents in the north-eastern corner of Romania, in Iaşi. He promised to get his staff to make the travel arrangements, making sure that my journey did not conflict with two parties he was arranging for me, to which – a rare breach of Foreign Office stuffiness, this – I was to ask anyone I wanted. I gave him a list of five or six dissidents I was particularly anxious to see, which he added to the half-dozen names I had already sent him from London.

Next day, a Saturday, I went to see Mariana Celac in an Embassy car supplied by Hugh and driven by a young woman just starting her diplomatic career, whose job was to keep an eye on me and learn something about dissidents. Mariana gave me a huge embrace at the door. She had the day well prepared. First we set off for the Romanian Orthodox monastery in Snagov, half an hour's drive away. It was the seventeenth centenary of the birth of Constantine, the first Christian Roman emperor, which the monks were celebrating with a remembrance service (as an absolute ruler over both Church and state, Constantine presumably appealed to Ceauşescu's warped sense of history). Inside the three-towered sixteenth-century church we became immediately immersed in the ritual, sitting among black-clothed peasants on crowded wooden benches in the candlelight. The singing, an ancient synthesis evolved over centuries, was richer and more powerful than Catholic services in Poland or Czechoslovakia. In spite of full-blown subservience to the Communist state, the Romanian Orthodox Church had preserved its austere musical and canonical unity with medieval Byzantium. I sat regretting how the Church of England had severed its links with its forebears, losing its monumental character and relying so much on spoken prayer.

Afterwards we filed through an archway to the monks' refectory, which was richly decorated with frescoes. In the kitchen, where the monks did their own cooking on a wood-burning ceramic stove, novices were slicing carrots, onions and potatoes and arranging them neatly in rows; outside, the vegetable garden was laid out in orderly lines. Evidently the old Romanian Orthodox tradition of working monks had survived the revolution.

We declined the monks' invitation to join them for lunch. I was intent on getting Mariana on her own, out of earshot and away from the bugging equipment that would almost certainly have been hidden in the car. Away, too, from the Embassy girl, even if this entailed some social embarrassment. Dividing the picnic Vanessa's cook had made for us, Mariana and I took our share through the orchard, making our way through deep uncut grass until we reached the side of a lake, where we sat down under an oak tree.

Shaded from the hot midday sun, Mariana began to unburden herself. Her life had changed for the worse since we had last seen each other. In poignant detail she described the kangaroo court to which she had been summoned after giving an interview to French television. As her office colleagues denounced her one by one, she found herself observing the proceedings with unexpected detachment. She could even see positive aspects to her ordeal: when she was placed under house arrest, her true friends emerged, visiting her every day, risking their own safety to improve her chances of avoiding some act of violence. The reason she was not in prison, she believed, was because she had not criticised Ceauşescu by name, but had confined herself to describing the living conditions in the country.

Some time after her demotion she had been given a job organising house repairs in Bucharest's poorest districts, where some of the most interesting buildings remained. She made it her aim to conserve as much original architectural detail as possible. In the course of her work she had uncovered, stacked away in a back room of the institute, a mass of ground plans and elevations of Bucharest's large-scale reconstruction in the 1920s and 1930s. Besides enjoying the research, she was relieved to be employed – which made her no longer subject to arrest as a 'parasite'.

I told her she could expect some helpful visitors during the summer: two architectural critics, Colin Amery and Gavin Stamp, who planned to write about Ceauşescu's Boulevard of Socialism and his 'systematisation' programme, and Tom Burke, the ecologist. She had done her homework. She brought with her three maps indicating the location of stretches of river killed by pollution, plus a top secret environmental report. I got these back to England through the diplomatic bag. But she did not really light up until I told her of the forthcoming visit of a parliamentary group from Westminster. I could see, without her having to spell it out, that she believed that the best prospect of change was through official links. She said that the British parliamentarians should especially ask to see nursery schools in new residential areas, where it would be impossible to disguise the conditions. When visiting orphanages, they should take note of the practice of enforced child labour. One week in three the orphans were sent to work in the fields.

Mariana had a disappointment in store for me. The 'time

was not yet right' for the Institute of Architecture to be offered a photocopier. I was more upset than I should have been that she had gone cold on the idea – I had had visions of her sneaking to the machine to copy leaflets or incriminating documents. It is a measure of the miasma of suspicion that infected Ceauşescu's Romania that the thought even flashed through my mind that the Securitate might have got to her. I should have realised that her 'show trial' had shaken her and made relations with her superiors impossible. Pressing her too hard, I wrung from her the tentative suggestion that one day, perhaps, we could send a photocopier through the auspices of the Church. I hoped that I would not find that Andrei Pleşu had also backed down.

We left the monastery garden and drove for two hours looking at destroyed, restructured villages. Mariana made sure we never stayed long. I would be liable to arrest if I looked inside any of the new houses, which I was much tempted to do. The fronts of those which lined the main road were adequately put together, but at the back and in the rows behind and out of sight large cracks were already appearing and rubble took the place of grass. At the village of Buftea, the largest battery hen farm settlement in Romania, a heavy storm made the road impassable. Temporarily trapped, we were sickened by the rising stench of chicken manure which permeated the car. What it must be like to live in Buftea did not bear thinking about.

Toward evening, back in Bucharest, Mariana and I parted and I asked the driver to drop me off. Then I went on foot to search out Nicu Steinhardt, an Orthodox monk, whom I knew from my Paris contacts to be on leave from his monastery in the Maramureş. He appeared at the door of his apartment on the third floor, a slight, bent figure clad in a red- and brown-striped silk dressing gown – clothes from the past. I felt as I had on first meeting Noica: a golden thread binding the present to the once civilised culture of pre-revolutionary Romania. Steinhardt's face lit up at the sight of a Western visitor. As for me, I fell for him straight away. He told me he was very old – sixty-seven.

When I looked surprised he corrected himself – seventy-six. His small square sitting room was crammed with books. To one side there was a bed covered by a woolly patterned Maramureş rug, and on the wall above his desk a picture of Solzhenitsyn and two photographs of Noica, together with a lighted candle burning under an icon of Jesus.

Vaguely related to Sigmund Freud, Steinhardt was descended from a prominent Jewish family in Bucharest. At some point – I am not sure when – he converted to Christianity. His uncompromising principles had condemned him to many years in prison, yet although conditions seemed to him as bad as they had been at the height of Gheorghiu-Dej's reign of terror in the 1950s, he was immune from the usual defeatist Romanian gloom. The previous year the Government had ordered a new census of Orthodox monasteries. He feared that this presaged a purge like that which had followed the survey of 1959, when the number of monks and nuns had been reduced from 7,000 to 2,000. Recently someone in his monastery had betrayed him and stolen one of his most secret manuscripts. Of course the Church was infiltrated and intimidated. Nevertheless, he believed that the younger generation of priests was strong and to be trusted. They flocked to his sermons, in which he pointedly avoided the sycophantic praise of the regime which was expected from the pulpit.

In earlier years Steinhardt had published several volumes of social and religious essays in the avuncular manner of G. K. Chesterton, extolling the individual confronted with the faceless force of technology and the state. He spoke several languages well, including English, and was so widely read that it was almost impossible to find a book that was new to him. His reading led him to share Noica's perception that Romanian culture, being anchored in European values, could never properly be considered in isolation, but he was powerless to combat the nationalist propaganda pumped out by the authorities, since he could never get anything published.

He confided in me that he might die any day. He had a heart

condition, and asked if I could get him some medicine. I learned later that his hypochondria was a standing joke in the dissident community. In prison some years before with Noica, the warders had made their usual search and found in his pockets nothing but tin after tin and jar after jar of pills and potions. I was able to tell him that Mark Almond would probably visit him in his monastery in July to bring him his prescription and to take his new manuscript to safety; Mark would also bring him the two much wanted books, Mircea Eliade's *La Moisson de Solstice* and *August 1917*, the only Solzhenitsyn he had not yet read. 'Mark Almond, Mark Almond,' he repeated like a mantra, intoning the gentle name, registering it as a symbol of England, medicine and civilisation. He agreed to write a short piece on present-day Romania for Mark to bring back to England. Much as he loved life he would not mind dying, he told me, now that his country and his beloved Bucharest had been all but destroyed.

I returned to the Arbuthnotts for supper. In all our conversations Hugh and I continued to communicate through gesture, allusion, notes and code. 'When the maid comes in with food,' I wrote in my diary, 'we alter our conversation still further. All the servants in the Ambassador's house are placed by the authorities in order to spy. They have been unable to employ staff of their own choice, but have to pick from a pre-selected group. It is not safe to speak in the garden because of laser equipment.'

Next day I telephoned Andrei Pleşu, whom I had not seen since our walk round Bucharest six months before. We met this time in his sturdy classical nineteenth-century house in the northern part of the capital. His wife, Catrinel, was having trouble with her eyes (virtually all the women in the area had an incurable eye infection which they attributed to demolition dust). Pleşu's ambitions were as lively as ever. With Liiceanu and a few others he wanted to produce a series of papers on guilt, censorship and subversion for us to smuggle out for publication in the West. To my relief, he was as keen as ever on getting the photocopier for the Institute of Arts – I suppressed the thought that its use might be limited to reproducing esoteric philosophical texts.

The Institute had been profoundly impressed by the National Gallery's offer and thrown into confusion as to how to respond. In the end Dr Manuela Cernat, the co-ordinating director, had written to Neil MacGregor thanking him for the generous gift 'with certitude that your kind gesture is the beginning of a fruitful dialogue. . . . We take the opportunity to express our hopes that the professional ties between the National Gallery and our institute will get stronger in the name and for the sake of our cultural goals, ever more vital, in this hasty end of century.' MacGregor had now caught the spirit of the whole thing and replied that 'an art historian scholar, Mark Thompson, MA, Cantab. (Hons), will be travelling to Romania to study further the works of Brancuşi and has undertaken to deliver the gift to you. We also enclose the publication *One Hundred Best Paintings*, which we hope will be of interest ...' In the same tone of fraternal cultural exchange, Pleşu fixed for me to go with him to the Union of Artists next day to seek an official invitation for me to return to Bucharest to exhibit my etchings.

That night was the first of the Arbuthnotts' two parties. At last I met Andrei Pippidi, about whom I had heard so much from Hugh Trevor-Roper and Mark Almond. As a grandson of the historian and former Prime Minister, Nicolae Iorga, Pippidi had protested vehemently at the plan to pull down his grandfather's house in Boulevard Ilie Pintilie. But the demolition had gone ahead in the summer of 1986, despite the fact that the mayor of Bucharest and the Institute of History (which still bore the Iorga name) had designed a project to have the house moved fifty metres. In an outraged letter Pippidi declared: 'The time comes when one learns to express aloud a protest thought out for a long time but never before uttered .... the blind mutilation of our city has to be halted.' Not until the letter had been rejected by all Romania's leading cultural journals did Pippidi allow Radio Free Europe to broadcast the text. So far no harm had come to him. Perhaps his high profile in England was shielding him from the revenge of the Securitate. Sitting on the sofa with me, he told me the whole story of Noica's last weeks, his funeral and the universal sense of bereavement caused by his death.

As the guests started to arrive – the Pleşus, Mariana Celac, the literary critic Eugen Simion and the Dutch ambassador Coen Stork – I was fascinated to see who else would feel able to turn up. I had been given the name of Ion Fistioc as a dissident. When I had worked out which he was, I went to talk to him, but found he was unable to speak German, French or English and could only communicate through an interpreter. Soon it became clear that his presence caused disquiet. He was muttered about in corners the whole evening. Who was he? Was he from the Securitate? 'The trouble is,' Pleşu eventually said, 'he is a peasant.'

Not being part of Bucharest's intellectual elite, Fistioc was a completely unknown quantity to the Embassy crowd, and as such highly suspect. In fact he was a very brave man, if startlingly naive. He had worked as an architect in a middle-ranking position in an economic ministry. Having observed that Romanians with Soviet contacts enjoyed a special status, he had written an open letter to the Soviet Embassy in Bucharest urging a U-turn in Romanian policy – a reduction in the export of food, a switch in supplies to home consumption and the making of appointments on the basis of professional competence. He had, of course, been immediately demoted and a short while later sacked. It was probably only an article about him in the *Free Romanian* and a mention on the BBC that inhibited the authorities from arranging his permanent disappearance.

I drove Mariana home. It would be the last I would see of her before I left for England. We talked about her husband Mihai Botez, with whom I had been corresponding intermittently, although I was not to meet him until I went to Washington later in the year. Botez was disillusioned at the West's lack of interest in Romanian oppression. He now saw clearly that the US State Department regarded dissidents as voices that distanced Ceauşescu from a close relationship with the USA, rather than as gallant friends of Western values. For this reason he had come round to arguing that whether or not to oppose the regime was not so much a matter of courage as a calculation of effectiveness: if intellectuals spoke out and were expelled, banished to internal exile or forced to emigrate, the benefit for society was nil. I could not guess how much Mariana agreed with her husband. She merely said as she left the car, 'Tell Mihai that I am strong and that it is important for me to remain so.'

The day after the party Pleşu and I set off for our meeting at the Union of Artists. Chaired by Ion Gheorghiu, the Foreign Affairs Secretary of the Fine Arts Union, and laboriously translated by an official interpreter, it felt interminable. I had brought out several of my etchings and some photographs of my paintings and felt foolishly flattered when Dan Haulica, editor of the quarterly journal *20th Century*, after inspecting my work, asked me to illustrate his next issue, which would be devoted to T. S. Eliot. (T. S. Eliot was a strange fish to have slipped through the censor's net: no doubt his brand of monarchical and religious conservatism was too obscure for them to understand.) The four or five men round the table peered at me continuously, quizzical and nervous. Quite soon Pleşu took control of the proceedings, steering the group to an agreement. I was to have a show at the Galeria Caminul Artei in the month of my choice next year. A secretary typed out the final points on exhibition costings. Grasping the top copy of the agreement I left triumphantly with Pleşu to inspect my designated gallery in the centre of Bucharest.

The Arbuthnotts' second party took place that evening – a lavish buffet for twenty. As with the first one, people sat in huddles, whispering on the stairs and in corners. A gaunt professor of architecture entered and for a time seemed frozen by the sight of two tables piled high with unheard of delicacies. A waiter broke the spell by handing him a glass of wine from a silver tray, whereupon he fell on the food like a starving man. I have an image of Pleşu and Liiceanu, stretching their legs out from the deep velvet sofa, arms clasped behind their necks, their eyes glinting amusedly at me, relaxed and at peace with themselves. I tackled Aurel Covaci of the Writers' Union (who according to Pleşu was there to report to the Securitate) to get him to invite Noel Malcolm, who was finishing his biography of the composer Georges Enescu, to talk about his book on his next visit to Romania. Covaci agreed. His unconcealed insincerity guaranteed that nothing would come of it.

Towards the end, I talked to Mircea Dinescu, the angry young man of Romanian poetry, whose physical strength and intensity of manner conveyed a ferocious charm. Some of his poems had been published in translation and as luck would have it I had read them. The density and ambiguity of much of his poetry provided him with a modicum of cover, but he did not flinch from portraying the realities of life. 'Indulgenta de Iarna (Cold Comfort)' was characteristic.

> God preserve me from those that want
> What's best for me,
> The nice guys
> Always ready to inform on me cheerfully -
> From the priest with a tape-recorder under his vestment
> And the blanket you can't get under without saying
> Good evening –
> From the dictator caught in the chords of the harp,
> From those angry with their own people.
> Now, when winter is drawing close,
> We have neither high walls
> Nor geese on the Capitoline,
> Only great provisions of tolerance and fear.

I glanced frequently at the door, hoping to see Radu Filipescu walk in. It was getting late and there was still no sign of him. Born into a family of high Party credentials, Filipescu

had been arrested in 1983, at the age of twenty-eight, for printing and distributing leaflets calling for a demonstration outside
the Central Committee building in Bucharest to demand
Ceauşescu's replacement. At his trial he was found guilty of
propaganda 'endangering the security of the state'. The defence
argued that Filipescu was exercising his right to peaceful freedom of expression, and that his sentence was a violation of the
Convention on Human Rights, ratified by Romania in 1974.
Two years into his ten-year prison sentence in the harsh maximum security prison of Aiud, Filipescu was released after being
named a Prisoner of Conscience by Amnesty International. The
authorities ordered him to apply for a passport and exit visa,
but he refused to leave the country, demanding reinstatement
at the state-owned Pipera Electronics complex.

Filipescu never arrived that night. Years later we met at a
Soros party in Bucharest, where he told me of his agitated state
of mind on receiving the ambassador's invitation. The invitation, delivered by hand, came at a time when he had just
restarted his dissident activities, printing 500 subversive leaflets
in his own home, which he left surreptitiously in shops. In
December, along with Mariana Celac, he had given an interview to French television. Once again he had been arrested and
interrogated but to his surprise released. During this new crisis
he proposed to his girlfriend, Daniela. He bought a smart blue
suit for himself and a short satin skirt for Daniela. Over a hundred wedding invitations had already been sent, when he found
a letter in his postbox. In his words,

> I read and re-read it. I had never received such a letter before
> – an invitation to the British Embassy to meet Jessica
> Douglas-Home ... the law restricting meetings with foreign-
> ers was trying to isolate us. Sometimes it succeeded. Daniela
> had been summoned to the Securitate and asked why she
> allowed me to meet with other women ... they told her that
> it was better for her not to risk her future alongside me. She
> is an anaesthetist working in an important hospital in

Bucharest and could have problems at work. This threat meant they could involve her or accuse her in the case when a patient died, even if she were not to blame ... Daniela did not show them that she was affected, but, once home, she started to cry as she was afraid a patient might die and she might be accused of being responsible.

I thought of what might happen if I go to the meeting at the Embassy. They will post another militia outside my house for a month. Maybe this would put off some guests but others would still come, in which case the atmosphere might be not too congenial. I did not know what useful results the Embassy meeting would produce. Discussions to which I could not have contributed or received useful information. Irrespective of the discussion, I would have easily been accused of treason and conspiracy with foreign forces for a long time. I had the feeling that the disadvantages of the meeting would have been greater than the advantages. With disappointment, but also with a feeling of revenge for lost freedom, I decided not to accept the invitation, telephoning the Embassy from a public callbox.

Hugh Arbuthnott had arranged for me to catch the overnight train to Iaşi, which was due to leave conveniently near the time the party was to end. At about ten o' clock Andrei Pleşu and Gabriel Liiceanu each drew me aside to tell me it was too dangerous for me to go north on my own. I saw their point but would have preferred them not to have spoken their thoughts aloud. I could not back out now. Hugh's assistant had made heroic efforts to get my reservations. He had been told that domestic flights to Iaşi were booked up for four days and that all the hotels were full. He had gone through a list of options – private car hire, the use of an Embassy car and driver and so on. Then somehow a breakthrough had occurred when, after several previous rejections, he managed to book a sleeper on the night train. If I were not to go now, these obstacles would have been overcome for nothing.

[172]

Adding to my anxiety, the maid who did my room had been asking questions about me and it was obvious that she had been through my personal belongings. Vanessa Arbuthnott had been angry with her. The maid had broken into tears. Hugh, too, now wondered whether I should go. But my bag was packed, ready beside me. With a pitying gaze from Andrei Pleşu, a reserved nod from Hugh and a look of sympathy from Vanessa, I was driven off to the station at 10.45 pm. The atmosphere was that of a family farewell as the soldier departs for the front.

From what I had read, Iaşi was a city about to erupt. With 24,000 students attending five institutes of higher education, it was the second largest university town in Romania, but the living conditions were the worst in the country. The pupils suffered from chronic food shortages, electricity cuts and freezing, unlit rooms. Reports had reached us that nearly 2,000 young men and women had paraded in the central square in March singing the Internationale. They had tramped on through the streets chanting patriotic songs and demanding 'water to wash and light to study'. In a panic, the County First Secretary had telephoned Bucharest for instructions, and had been ordered to provide electricity and hot water immediately. Two days later a Securitate team had been sent to find the ringleaders, but without result: the march had been spontaneous.

Perversely, I was looking forward to getting out of Bucharest. I wanted to get a wider feel for Romania. The train was comfortable, the sheets clean. I settled on the top bunk, lay down and wrapped round my chest the long leather strap holding my handbag. As the train began to move out of the station, the door opened and a pretty woman with immaculate shining hair and make-up, dressed in a chic suit, slithered into our narrow compartment. Hidden as she was in the bunk below, I could not catch another glimpse at her, but I read for a bit, resolving anyway to keep the light on. Soon I dropped off to sleep. Perhaps an hour later my eyes flickered open. Parallel to my face, only inches away, the woman's eyes were staring intently at me. I let out a piercing scream, then another.

'Doown't bee afraayyed' she drawled twice in a voice of sinister menace. She returned to her bunk, and the light went off. To this day I do not know what she was doing. Maybe she was merely having a good look at the target to whom she had been assigned; maybe she was looking for my Romanian addresses. It crossed my mind that she might have been the same woman who had met me at the airport when I first arrived in Romania.

The next morning, 4 May, I arrived in Iaşi very tired. The elegant woman of the previous night had slipped away from the compartment during the early hours. In her place a student with remarkably good English came up to me on the platform, trying to befriend me, offering to help. I shook him off and found my own way to the centre of town. The greasy coffee in the main hotel took an hour and a half to appear. Meanwhile, I laid out in front of me my bits of coded paper and my street map, finally settling on a visit to the writer Dan Petrescu, who had given an interview to the French daily *Libération* earlier in the year. Like Cornea, Petrescu had appealed for a moral regeneration based on an alliance between workers and intellectuals.

It was a short tram ride. As I climbed the concrete stairs of the central apartment bloc in a dilapidated 1950s building I heard, on reaching the first landing, a fast-moving heavy tread of boots coming up behind me. I whipped round to find myself looking into the face of a Securitate officer. I dashed by him back down the stairs, out through the door and on to a tram, which miraculously was waiting a few yards away, pumping and hissing out air.

I disembarked near Iaşi University and walked up the steps towards the imposing façade and into the hall to search for Thomas Barzin, a lecturer from France who, Pleşu had told me, was on a year's assignment in the language department. At a loss where to find him, I asked for help from a young student, who led me out to another wing, talking as fast as anyone I had ever known. He was in the fourth year of an electronics course, but launched immediately into a discussion of European literature, questioning me on the finer points of Kafka. So engrossed were we that I failed to see the figure of another Securitate officer, who now rudely blocked our path, demanding our passports. With a grunt, mine was returned, but not the student's, who was told to report immediately to the police station. I was haunted for months by anxiety that because of me the student's future might have been ruined. But there was nothing I could do until I returned to Bucharest, where I made a formal complaint through the French and British Embassies.

Not for the first time I reflected how each encounter with a dissident, however truncated, forged a bond of friendship, or something greater than friendship, out of the danger of the occasion. This was above all true of Romanians, who were dicing with their lives in even talking to a foreigner. Furious with the world, I carried on to the French department, where I was shown into the office of the departmental head. With a look of naked antagonism she asked me to leave immediately, shouting out for all to hear, first in good English and then even more loudly in Romanian, that I should never have been allowed into the building. The Securitate had won. They had prevented me from talking to anyone and I was reduced to examining the veneer of the city. I spent the remaining time looking in the empty shops, observing the people and going into the churches of Trei Ierarhi and Sfântu Nicolae Domnesc. The hotel was filthy and its food nauseated me, so after two days I left for Bucharest by the morning train.

The long journey by rail was to prove invaluable. Not least, it obliterated my sense of failure. Conversations with strangers in trains and planes generally give me claustrophobia, as hours planned for uninterrupted reading evaporate into trivia. But a tall, well-built engineer from Iaşi with a consuming interest in racing cars was persistent. Something about this man set him apart from the surrounding world of intrigue. It was a remarkable characteristic of the oppression that it brought people's moral nature into sharp relief. Quite suddenly, in a crowd of worn grey faces, or in the most ordinary queue of weary scavengers, you saw the face of a selflessness, all the more striking in that it expected no acknowledgement. Where hopes could only be private, spiritual energy seemed to intensify because it could find no release in the sympathy of a fellow sufferer.

So it was with my encounter with Victor Grădinariu. He addressed me as though sent from on high for my salvation, his brown eyes lit by a childlike interest. He was offended by the title of the book on my lap – *Memoirs of an Anti-Semite* by von Rezzori. He was determined that I should explain myself, and as I tried to do so, he watched me with a kind of intimate concern. I tried to explain von Rezzori's irony; then I continued talking, covering all kind of topics that I would never have dreamed of discussing with a stranger in England, let alone in Romania. He responded in kind, and after a few minutes I realised what nuggets of gold he was offering me in his broken English. Indeed, I owed much of my understanding of everyday Romanian life in the 1980s to this one train journey with Victor Grădinariu.

In his thirties, married and with a young daughter, Grădinariu was travelling to Bucharest to visit his brother. His only luggage rested on the rack above us – ten bottles of wine, to be used for barter. Although his wife, Luminiţa, was a teacher, Grădinariu's was a world of factory and building workers, of an Iaşi acquaintance imprisoned for denouncing Ceauşescu in the street, of families scrounging, stealing and informing to keep their children from starvation. His sister-in-law had wanted to distribute pamphlets demanding Ceauşescu's overthrow, but had been dissuaded – at least for the time being – by the rest of the family. 'No one in Romania will die for his country. There is no hope,' he muttered. 'We are hungry all the time. No meat, no butter, no eggs, no cheese, no milk...' As he spoke he glanced constantly round the carriage, trying to identify informers. They averted their eyes. To me they all looked equally suspicious.

Despite everything, Grădinariu held out some hope. He had

come to know three Americans in Iaşi during the last year. One had written a novel of his experiences, which was being broadcast in instalments on Radio Free Europe. Surely this way the West would be alerted to the Romanians' misery? I could see that he thought that I too must take on the role of saviour. On parting I gave him Olivia Manning's *Balkan Trilogy*, which I had hoped to finish before he had interrupted me. Under its cover I slipped a £50 note. Not for him, I teased, but for his sister-in-law to print her pamphlets. When we met again in 1990 he told me that he had wrestled with his conscience to restrain himself from buying the one thing he most wanted in this world – an engine for a rough-track racing car. For two years the £50, worth two months' salary in Romania, lay untouched in his bank before finding its way to his relative.

I had a last lunch with Mircea Dinescu and his wife, Maria, in their villa close to the Pleşus. It was strange that he had not yet been expelled from the Writers' Union and was able to keep his newspaper job on the *Romania Libera*. No doubt the key to his protection, as so often in Romania, was the Moscow connection – his wife, a professional translator, was Russian. Dinescu was to play a prominent role in the uprising in Bucharest in December 1989.

My final call was to say goodbye to Hugh Arbuthnott. As I entered his room, he rose from his desk and beckoned me to follow him. We descended the main staircase and went through a side door down into the cellars of the Embassy building, unlocking more and more doors with Hugh's heavy key until we came to a bare room with a table and two chairs. The scene was out of a John le Carré spy thriller. In the security of the bug-free chamber, Hugh's personality was transformed. 'Sit down,' he said relaxedly 'and don't tell anyone in London or anywhere else about this room. We are now free to talk...' With black humour we assessed Romania's situation together. Perhaps he hoped that I had more to tell him than I did. I impressed on him the incident with the student in Iaşi and hoped he would complain. When we parted, we promised each other that in our different ways we would do everything we could to expose the inhuman decree that allowed the police to arrest a Romanian for talking to a foreigner and to persuade international opinion that it constituted a heinous infringement of the Helsinki Accord.

The only gift I could think of for Vanessa and Hugh was my treasured photocopy of Patrick Leigh Fermor's introduction to Matila Ghika's out-of-print *The World Mine Oyster*. I knew the Arbuthnotts would appreciate Leigh Fermor's poetic portrait of the old hierarchical Romania, as he had witnessed it during its last summer in 1939.

Seventeen

Romania was now widely seen as the most sinister country of the Soviet bloc, and academics were increasingly reluctant to visit. It was usually the wives who put their foot down. I should have been more sympathetic. In *Red Horizons* Pacepa had given an unforgettable account of the state apparatus of terror and although it was fashionable in intellectual circles to accuse him of exaggerating, when the time came to book a flight to Bucharest the thought tended to surface that perhaps his accounts of 'radiation guns' and other instruments of murder might after all be true. Mark Almond, however, was fearless and agreed to return to Romania in the summer of 1988. This allowed me time to visit Poland and Czechoslovakia (and later in the summer, for the first time, Russia).

The contrast with Romania was extraordinary. Warsaw was teeming with social and political groupings of every colour. People no longer spoke in hushed voices and could write more or less what they wanted. All the same, the atmosphere was volatile – a strange blend of fear and excitement. No one knew the limits of the changes that Moscow would tolerate. During Gorbachev's state visit earlier in July, he had overtly supported Jaruzelski, evidently approving of the tactic of bringing Solidarity into the tent and laying the ground for all-party discussions. But Soviet policy seemed to be an improvisation. There was no visible master plan. Sooner or later the situation would spin out of control.

In Prague the old guard held its grip, but the cracks to which Bratinka had referred three years earlier were now deep crevices. The absence of fear produced its own sense of liberation. Hejdánek had changed completely from when I first met him.

'Younger, cheerful, lively and pain-free,' I wrote in my diary, adding 'but this energy was a common denominator I was to find, without exception, in everyone I met during this stay.' On my second day I met Alena and Petr Pithart and went straight to Cardinal Tomášek's palace to seek an audience. Alena waited with me in the ante-room, while Petr Pithart addressed a long queue of Czechs and Slovaks bearing petitions, pleading with them to give me precedence and explaining to them my mission to halt the destruction of the churches in Romania.

Within minutes I was allowed to the top of the line and was ushered in to a large panelled room, where the Cardinal, robed in a long black garment with red piping, red lining and a red sash, quietly received me. He heard my story in French and went over to his desk, to a tall 1940s typewriter. He said with sadness that he was unable to 'interfere in a matter internal to Romania', but began slowly, elegantly and laboriously to type out a simple message of prayer for the Romanian people, which he signed. Then he took out from his desk a black and white postcard of himself, his hand raised in blessing on his palace balcony. This, too, he signed and gave to me. I left the room elated. An old peasant woman, who had risen at 1 am to travel from her Slovak village to Prague for an audience, asked Alena if we were Catholics. There was dismay on her crumpled face when she learned I was a Protestant. Alena pulled out her gold cross from beneath her jumper to show that we were Christians, but the woman's troubled look remained.

Bratinka had not yet left with his family for their country cottage and was free to take me on a trip he had long promised me – to the castle at Karlštejn, the St John of the Rock monastery and on into the Sudetenland, to the stricken mining area around Most. After the beauty of the first part of our journey we bumped along for two hours in his little car, stopping for greasy soup in a hideous concrete building in Roudnice. On the last lap, I was so engrossed in Bratinka's conversation that I noticed only flashes of the high-summer green of the Czech countryside.

Suddenly Bratinka stopped in a lay-by to take me, he said, for a walk in a wood. I opened the car door to look around; but it was no longer summer and there was no wood. No blossom, or buds. No leaves. Nothing green. Skeletons, yes, with thick grey spines and jagged legs and arms, stretching out to me in their thousands with the suffering, wounded pride of thalidomide victims. I looked closer at the dead trees. I touched their grey bark, and touched the ground. In silence we wandered up a slope to the highest point and looked down into a vast hole of rubble and bricks that had once been the town of Most. Hundreds of its buildings had been demolished in the 1970s. A historic cathedral had been moved a few hundred yards on rollers. The air was now so polluted that children were issued masks before setting off to school. Some days the radio warned people not to leave their houses at all. There was an appalling rate of morbidity and birth defects in babies.

Bratinka gestured towards Germany, visible on the horizon. The toxic air had spread its desolation all the way to the border. Mile after mile of stricken stumps were broken and bent double, or stood forlornly in lines or clusters. The scene was like a First World War battlefield. It brought back to me a haunting childhood memory of the poisoned world prophesied by Rachel Carson in *Silent Spring*. Bratinka had been here many times and was used to the sight. But our mood changed and we left soon for home.

Later he wrote to me:

I want to tell you about my sorrow and my joy. The sorrow is caused by the fact that your stay was so short and the joy by having had the first opportunity in years to speak with you alone for some hours without any interruptions and distractions. However, some important themes we only scratched on their surface, and some others we left out altogether.

Meanwhile, after a day or two in Bucharest, Mark Almond

had left to seek out Doina Cornea in Cluj. Our most recent information was that she was under surveillance at home, looking after her ailing elderly mother. Her last prison spell, after the Braşov riots, had been relatively brief. Three years into *perestroika* and *glasnost*, the treatment of dissidents throughout the Soviet bloc had become erratic and public demonstrations of support for Cornea in Paris, London and Geneva had no doubt contributed to her release.

Mark walked unaccosted down the street, through a little gate and up a garden path. Cornea herself opened her front door and let him in to the hall. Silently assessing him, anxious to discover how trustworthy this stranger might be, she led him into her sitting room, where her mother lay in the corner, huddled in bed under a rug, oblivious to her surroundings.

During the two-hour exchange which followed, in sign language, notes and monosyllabic French, Mark found Cornea utterly resolute. She was astonished that he had not been picked up by the surveillance team posted at the end of her street. Nevertheless, his visit presented her with the opportunity she had been waiting for. As he was leaving, she took a small envelope from its hiding place and slipped it into his hand. 'Tell the BBC not to use this until after Ariadne's visit in August,' she whispered. Ariadne was Cornea's daughter who had emigrated to Paris.

Mark headed for the centre of the town to look for a hotel with a cloakroom. Once there, he opened the envelope. In minute, condensed script on fine tissue paper, Cornea had penned a 1,000-word open letter to Ceauşescu demanding that he abandon the destruction of Romania's 13,000 villages and denouncing the Communist Party's entire post-war collectivisation programme. Speaking from the heart in direct response to daily life, she wrote not so much of the material hardship suffered by Romanians as of the spiritual devaluation of the society.

... Try to imagine the grief of these people driven out of

their homes, from their villages. Human beings are not objects. A human settlement is not a random conglomeration of blocks inhabited by impersonal creatures, gathered together by chance. A village is a spiritual community which has grown over the centuries. It is the love of people for their land and for the house in which they were born. A village is the graveyard where their parents are buried. The church – sometimes several hundred years old and often preserved by a miracle from the scourge of the Turks – is the church in which they were married, in which they baptised their children and in which they prayed in times of trial...

Leaving the hotel, Mark walked straight to the station, determined to take the first train out of the country. Within an hour he was on his way to Budapest, crammed into a smoke-filled compartment between elderly Transylvanian peasants clutching empty nylon bags. At the Hungarian border the train juddered to a stop in a series of jerky spasms. This was the moment he had been dreading. Through the window he could see grey-uniformed officials on the platform. After a long wait, with the noise of opening and shutting doors getting ever nearer, there was a commotion in the passageway as an old Romanian woman whose papers were not in order was pushed out onto the platform, where she wept alone and bereft. Then, ripping the sliding door back hard into its socket, the police reached Mark's compartment. The other inhabitants were ordered out. As they left, a woman shouted at Mark over her shoulder in a harsh, sneering voice, 'If the rules were abided by, none of this would happen.'

Two policemen entered, drew the curtains and told Mark to remove his clothes. Through a crack in the brown, flimsy material of the curtains he could see a blue-suited plain clothes Securitate officer on the platform, masterminding the search from a distance. Having stripped him down to his stockinged feet, they took away his roll of camera film, his Romanian newspaper

Scânteia, and Andrei Pleşu's recent, legally printed, book on modern philosophy. On this first search the police found nothing. From outside on the platform orders came for a second, rougher search. Finally, having again drawn a blank, they gave up.

Mark dressed. The one place the police had not looked was in his socks. He had folded Cornea's tissue-paper letter into a one-inch oblong strip. And despite its unconventional hiding place, Cornea's minuscule text, written like some ancient hieroglyphics, was none the worse for wear. The compartment filled up again and the train moved on into Hungary. On arrival in London, he handed over Cornea's letter to Radio Free Europe and the BBC World Service who, abiding by her request concerning the date of its release, transmitted it to the West and into Eastern Europe in September. At the same time the text appeared in *Le Monde* and the *Spectator* (along with an anonymous editorial 'Remember Romania').

Cornea's words proved to be an unexpectedly powerful weapon. An academic and a Christian, she became for Romania what Aleksandr Solzhenitsyn was for the wider underground resistance movement. As her letters were broadcast, many of them short essays in their own right, her stature as a truly heroic dissident grew. Her writing and her suffering focused the attention of the world on Romania's tragedy. At the Eminescu Trust we had long admired Cornea's stand, and it was her attack on the destruction of the villages[1] which gave us the idea for the *Campaign for the Protection of Villages in Romania*, which was to get off the ground in London a few months later.

The publicity given to Cornea's predicament in France encouraged Danièle Mitterrand, wife of the French President, to invite her to a human rights conference to be held during the

---

[1] Cornea wrote a second letter on the same theme, taken out by Josie Dubie who made the documentary *Red Disaster* for Belgian television, broadcast on Romania's National Day.

bicentenary celebrations of the French Revolution. But after the broadcast of her letter smuggled by Mark, she was placed under house arrest and of course denied a passport by the Romanian authorities.

A month later it was Noel Malcolm who took his summer holiday break in Romania. His report opened: 'August 1988. Overall my trip was a washout – cut short by severe illness after a few days. I saw only three people: Celac, Pippidi and a friend of Pippidi's.' Looking back, it is a miracle that more of us did not fall ill. On Noel's first day he had a filthy room 'with cockroaches everywhere'. He did not record where or what he ate, but clearly on that first evening he had food poisoning.

Leaving the bulk of his visits in Bucharest until after his trip to the north, Noel nevertheless reported that Pippidi was well, that they had discussed his work on Western attitudes to the Ottoman Empire in the sixteenth and seventeenth centuries, and that Noel had had the unpleasant task of asking him to inform Pleşu of the seizure of Pleşu's book by the Securitate on the Hungarian border. He left 'a jar of Colman's English mustard by special request, as well as Trevor-Roper's latest book and one on the French Revolution'.

Noel's first twinges of nausea hit him during the flight to Iaşi, but he was just able to search out Professor Alexandru Zub, renowned for his editions of the classic ninteenth- and early twentieth-century Romanian historians, at his institute in the Boulevard Karl Marx. Much of Zub's early adult life had been spent in prison; now he specialised in historiography:

Very likeable, very thoughtful man; fine-boned, broad-browed, Slavic sort of face, like a Czech or a Pole. My presence at his institute (admittedly as a history don from Cambridge) was obviously not thought problem-causing: he showed me round and introduced me to people in every room. After lunch I had 15 minutes with him in his study. I broached the question of the regime's hatred for the past, and we began to have a serious discussion. He said he was full of despair – also the West must take a lot of responsibility, having given Ceauşescu legitimacy at a crucial time. 'At first legitimacy came from the Red Army. Then it came from the Stalinist myth of industrial progress. Then, just as everyone stopped believing in that, Ceauşescu got it from walking round on the world stage, visiting the White House and Buckingham Palace.' He didn't say so directly, but he seemed to think that making Ceauşescu a pariah internationally would still be a powerful weapon, even now.

Dragging himself further north by bus, Noel managed to visit the birthplace of Georges Enescu, the subject of his biography in hand, before finally collapsing in bed in the town of Suceava – 'vomiting, diarrhoea, stomach cramps, splitting headache, high fever, shivering, complete loss of physical strength, difficulty in standing up'.

After two days of near oblivion he somehow got himself back to Bucharest and, clearly not improving, bought a ticket to London for the following day. He made one last effort:

> After a couple of hours in bed, went to see Mariana Celac. She was well; said the books had arrived safely, and were just what she wanted...I left all my remaining Lei: 4,400. This is equivalent to two months' wages for the average Romanian... she offered to act as a bank for future visitors, but I insisted that she should not get involved in any to-ing and fro-ing of money with foreigners – that's the first sort of thing the Securitate would try to pin on her anyway. I told her to spend it on herself or anyone she knew that really needed it.

Leaving Mariana Celac's apartment, he moved on to a final meeting but noticed almost immediately that he was being followed by a Securitate police car. After a short while he found himself too weak to throw it off:

> I walked to a main street, got on a tram, travelled one stop and started to walk back. It was only half a mile but I was

walking at about 1 mph and feeling rather faint. By the time I got back to square one it was dark...I thought I would simply not have the strength to walk back again from there. So I caught a bus back into the centre of town. Sorry this sounds so feeble. At the time of writing, five days later and after rehydration therapy, I'm still having difficulty walking up stairs.

On returning to England Noel was diagnosed as having a virulent form of dysentery special to Eastern Europe. He spent several days in hospital and did not finally recover until five or six weeks later.

Another desperate winter in Romania set in. During the bitter cold and snow of mid-November 1988, Leszek Kolakowski's daughter, Agnieszka, a Cambridge philosophy graduate living in Paris, agreed to go to Bucharest for us. Aged twenty-eight, she was small but not frail, with an appealing (and for me very paintable) face. I loaded her up in London with a mass of philosophy and history books which she crammed into her hand luggage.

Agnieszka was at a stage in her life when she was rediscovering her Jewish roots. Her first day she went to look at the synagogue in Calea Călărasilor. The southern side of the street had been bulldozed from Piaţa Unirii as far as the eye could see. To the east she saw mostly rubble, guarded by soldiers against looting, and occasionally an abandoned old house, the courtyard strewn with rubbish, the wrought iron gates broken and askew, the decaying wreck obviously next in line for the demolition which progressed inexorably house by house and street by street . The entrance of the synagogue was guarded. When she tried to walk in, a beefy-faced man emerged from his post and demanded her passport, insisting that she needed a guide and refusing to divulge the times of services. Then he brusquely marched her in and out in two minutes flat.

Back at her hotel, she stuffed a dozen or so books into her carrier bag and set off north to see the Pleşus, walking to Piaţa

Aviatorilor and doubling back through the park, where she wandered or sat until about six o'clock.

The street was empty and I was about to go in when a couple walked past me and entered the gate. By then I had passed the house twice and did not think it prudent either to go away and do it again or to dawdle outside any longer, so I went in after them...I was surprised when the man turned around, barred my way, and asked menacingly who I was and what I wanted and who I was coming to see ... I said feebly I was looking at the old houses, whereupon he said, 'Go away, this is not a museum.' . . . I apologised and went outside ... He poked his head out and said, quite angrily by now, 'Why are you still here? What are you doing? What do you want? Go away.' ... I went, quite frightened by then.

Of course this was Pleşu. He thought Agnieszka Kolakowska was a policewoman; she thought he was the Securitate. Luckily she was able to see the Dinescus next day, who cleared up the matter.

The first thing they asked me was whether I was the mad woman the Pleşus had told them about that morning; they had compared notes, in some bewilderment, because I had compounded the confusion by speaking briefly on the telephone to the Dinescus, who thought I was Jessica and rang up the Pleşus, and by then none of them knew what to think...he was very glad of the books, especially the Auden; he was touched that Jessica remembered that Auden was his favourite poet...

Mircea Dinescu told Agnieszka that things were grim and getting grimmer by the week. He was still a Party member with hopes, which he increasingly saw to be delusions, of reforming the structure from the inside. He and Pleşu had recently tried unsuccessfully to organise a letter of protest against censorship, the law on talking to foreigners and the destruction of the villages. The meeting in his house had, of course, been bugged,

[188]

and he was 'invited for a talk', threatened with expulsion from the Party and warned that he might be accused of high treason (this carried a penalty of life imprisonment, but the charge was rarely invoked and Dinescu did not take it very seriously). On the other hand, if he cooperated he could be helped in various ways, his life made easier on a personal level.

Agnieszka plodded back to the Pleşus in a blizzard, feeling jittery. Her suitcase, heavy with books, and the fact that she was bundled up in a scarf, with a snow-filled gale behind her, made it impossible to see if anyone was following her without actually stopping and turning in an obvious way. But Pleşu opened the door and they were able to joke about their first tense encounter. He pounced on the books, particularly the Greek New Testament. When it dawned on him that Agnieszka was Leszek Kolakowski's daughter, he got down on his knees and said he would have to change into his best suit.

He had been exhausted, he said, on Friday night because he had flown into a rage at the institute that day and ranted quite openly about conditions in Romania, especially the law on foreigners, which he found painful and humiliating. Pressure had been brought to bear on each of them individually at work to sign a document acknowledging this law and promising to report any foreign contacts. They all refused to sign.

He referred ruefully to the meeting at the Dinescus' house when about eight of them had failed to agree on the text of a letter of protest. Some were reluctant to sign anything. He confessed to what he called a 'Polish complex'. They were not as brave or as organised as the Poles; they did not want to be professional dissidents, they merely wanted to get on with their lives; but the normal business of getting on with life was already a political choice, foisted upon them against their will. And, having become politicised, they had nowhere to channel their political energies, no movements to lead. Any protests, even on the smallest scale, brought immediate reprisals. There was nothing they could do; they felt completely isolated.

Pleşu told Agnieszka that he had developed a strong interest in Judaism, which he felt was indispensable to an understanding of Christianity. He asked for any books or commentaries on the Talmud, on mysticism, Maimonides, etc. He was, she wrote,

> grateful for Jessica's phone call; it helps them, he says, to be rung up from time to time, to show those who are listening that there is interest in them in the West. His name in the papers, as a scholar, of course, not as anything else, might also provide them with some additional safety. ...There is nothing we can do in the sense of helping or trying to create any kind of structured opposition movement: for the time being all we can do is come to see them, and talk, and bring books... In spite of the nervousness and apprehension, and grim prospect for the future, they are determined not to be afraid, but to meet as many foreigners as possible. I was amazed at the normality and ease with which they welcomed me and spoke with me ... I left them around 9, feeling that if I had been arrested as I left their house it would have been more than worth it and they, for their part, said as much.

There was a refrain in Pleşu's, in Dinescu's, and indirectly in Liiceanu's conversation about this time which conveyed a sense of guilt at their compliance with the regime, at their failure to move from dissent to outright dissidence. It cannot have arisen out of our attitude, for as their trial of courage grew our respect for them if possible increased, especially since we knew how much they would have preferred to remain in their ivory tower, remote from politics.

Perhaps Pleşu had been stung by recent criticism from a Romanian exile in America who belittled his and Liiceanu's preoccupation with abstract philosophy, on the grounds that it bore no relevance to the current tragedy. They knew that philosophy could never solve the problem of the meat supply, but nevertheless it was their duty, as good disciples of Noica, to expose the falsity of the regime's propaganda.

So careful had Agnieszka been, so many precautions had she taken, that she was sure she had not been followed. She was therefore shocked by her reception at the airport.

At the customs they were waiting for me; no one else was searched. They examined all the linings and took away my passport, ticket, map, addresses of British and French Embassies (but nothing else) and camera. I was then strip searched by a very polite woman who apologised that her hands were cold; coat lining, shoes, everything was examined (I am not sure about the socks because they came off with my shoes, which were falling apart)...After about half an hour two men – one uniformed, one plain-clothed – approached and asked whether I had ever been to Romania before, what was a woman doing alone in Bucharest in the middle of winter, I must tell the truth etc...I was then politely asked to join the plain-clothed man in a little room furnished with chairs 'where we can be more comfortable' and a coffee was brought to me. He said 'You have committed grave crimes against the Socialist Republic of Romania, crimes for which you would have long been arrested were it not for our good relations with France, and our wish to maintain them.' Throughout all this I remained uncomprehending and asked repeatedly to be told what crimes I had committed. The response was always, 'We know exactly what you have done; you have done terrible things, but I won't go into details.' ... A frequent line was, 'You must tell your patron that we in the Socialist Republic of Romania will not tolerate this kind of thing.' He then repeated several times that I would never be allowed back to the Socialist Republic of Romania, returned my things and let me go.

Agnieszka was right: she had not been followed. Instead her entire four-hour conversation with the Pleşus had been bugged. In 1997 I was able to check her story by reading the Securitate account, which runs to twelve pages. Some passages of the Securitate text appear jumbled but nothing is fabricated; indeed it is striking for its dispassionate, almost scholarly tone. I could not help being flattered by its reference to myself as 'a very dangerous lady' – 'O *doamnă foarte periculoasă*'; but it was chilling even in retrospect to see the casual way in which Pleşu assumed that inconvenient foreigners were liable to 'physical disappearance'.

Eighteen

As 1988 drew to its dismal end, reports were coming in of hundreds of refugees fleeing Romania every day, seeking asylum in Hungary. William Waldegrave, the new Minister of State at the Foreign Office, took a tough stand on human rights abuse in the Warsaw Pact countries. His sympathy for the dissidents' cause was the equal of Malcolm Rifkind's. We briefed him about Doina Cornea, and he made frequent interventions on her behalf. He also had our full list of dissidents in Prague.

In Czechoslovakia, too, the Foreign Office had discovered a sudden enthusiasm for our friends. Pithart, Havel and Bratinka found themselves fêted by the British Embassy.

> On Sunday October 23rd [Bratinka wrote to me] I dined with five British MPs. Early on the morning of October 27th I was taken in prison where I spent four hours with more than a hundred other 'dissidents'. Half an hour after I arrived home from prison I sat down to read your letter. And I am writing these lines after I returned from an interrogation concerning The Movement of Civil Rights. So you see I am in an acute danger of forgetting the meaning of that already almost alien word 'boredom'.

Meanwhile, in mid-November, Silviu Brucan travelled to London bringing with him a paper on 'the crisis of Communism' which he planned to deliver at whatever academic institution would have him. This devious old Party veteran had suffered little since his criticism of Ceauşescu over the Braşov riots. Although he had been 'under surveillance' he apparently had no difficulty in obtaining visas for travelling abroad. From London he went on to Moscow. He was later to claim that he was received there by Gorbachev, who told him that the Kremlin favoured the overthrow of Ceauşescu on condition that it was engineered so as to leave the Communist Party in control. (Little as we trusted Brucan, this seemed a credible account.[1]) Brucan arranged Soviet protection for himself on his return to Romania; the Bucharest correspondent of *Pravda* was ordered to visit his house at regular intervals.

To keep Doina Cornea in the limelight, I enlisted the support of Norman Stone and his wife Christine's first husband, the campaigning journalist Christopher Booker, for a letter to *The Times*. 'The Romanian authorities have let it be known that continued interest in the fate of Doina Cornea ... will damage relations between our two countries ...This threat should be turned on its head: ...We believe it is the British Government who should insist that relations cannot continue in the face of such brutality.' We also called on the Queen to withdraw the honorary knighthood she had bestowed on Ceauşescu and return the Star of Romania, and suggested that the Royal Society of Chemistry should revoke the honours it had given to Elena Ceauşescu.

In the event, it was not until the following year that ministers on behalf of the Queen, with what seemed to me embarrassing timing, stripped Ceauşescu of his title just as he was about to flee his palace. That this decision was taken at all was probably a result of pressure from Prince Charles. His understanding of the suffering generated by Communist regimes was by no means new, perhaps influenced by his friendship with Laurens van der Post. In a speech in Canada in 1983 he had gone far beyond the traditional royal platitudes to plead for Western support for those enduring life under totalitarian rule. In September 1984 he had written to me about my paper on Peace Studies that had so enraged the academics:

...Laurens has just sent me a copy of your paper... I <u>so</u> agree

1 S. Brucan, 'Intilnirea secreta Brucan-Gorbaciov', *Evenimentul Zilei*, 19 November 1992.

with you that most of these people are approaching peace from the wrong end, as it were. You cannot stop wars by trying to abandon weapons because, as I see it, there will always be people who are dangerous or evil enough to use them against you for their own psychological reasons. You are <u>absolutely</u> right about <u>individual</u> freedom – especially spiritual freedom – & that true peace comes about when conditions allowing that freedom are allowed to prevail. Why is it that so many people seem unwilling or unable to hear the anguished cries of those who do live in a state of 'graveyard tranquillity'?...

He had become increasingly concerned about Ceauşescu's regime in Romania. He had been given Pacepa's *Red Horizons* and I sent him some more recent material, which shocked him deeply.

After pressing hard for a stronger British policy stand and failing to get anything but complacent stonewalling out of the Foreign Secretary, Geoffrey Howe, Prince Charles started to explore the possibilities of making a major speech on Romania. For this he needed independent advice. At the request of one of his private secretaries, David Wright, who had been seconded to him from the Foreign Office, I suggested five East European experts who I was confident would give him an accurate and full account of the Romanian scene – Noel Malcolm, Mark Almond, George Urban, Christopher Booker and the Sandhurst Soviet military expert Christopher Donnelly.

Meeting at King's Cross station one early January afternoon, we set off to Sandringham on the King's Lynn train. I have a vivid memory of an uproarious journey, during which we tried without much success to agree on some unified suggestions for the Prince. I was aghast at George Urban's draft speech, repeatedly dragging in 'our global village' and 'our common European home'. From the moment Gorbachev first began to use these phrases I saw them as a part of a propaganda drive to assimilate the Soviet Union into the European Community and

I was in no doubt that they would dismay our allies in Romania.

Arriving at the station at 4 pm, we were met by a dark-suited equerry with a Range Rover, which accommodated us all in comfort except Mark, who volunteered to squeeze in the back behind the bars of a partition for royal corgis. Over the most delicate of teas at Sandringham, we mused over our range of options. I had hoped that Prince Charles might like the idea of a visit to Romania, using as a pretext the tomb of his great-great-grandmother, Countess Rhedey, which lay in the village of Sângiorgiu de Pădure in northern Romania. Since the village was among those scheduled for demolition, it would serve our purpose well.

Prince Charles wondered where on earth he could find in his already crowded timetable the right occasion to attack Ceauşescu without its appearing too contrived. Anything overtly political was, for a member of the Royal Family, out of bounds. On the other hand, anything connected to architecture would be acceptable. We each agreed to write a mock speech from which Prince Charles could lift material for his own text. I was to act as the focus and forwarding agent. Within a fortnight the Foreign Office gave clearance for a speech, but his private secretary wrote to me that a royal visit to the ancestral tomb was impossible.

Meanwhile in Romania Hugh Arbuthnott was not letting matters rest. Early in January 1989 he made plans to call on Doina Cornea privately in Cluj. Embassy staff were instructed to inform the Ministry of Foreign Affairs of his intention to meet local officials in Cluj. There was to be nothing furtive about his visit: on the other hand he did not intend to give forewarning to the Romanian authorities. After all – under the Helsinki Accords – there could hardly be a legitimate objection to a call on a Romanian citizen living at home who had been convicted of no crime. Nevertheless, for a career diplomat, it was a bold and unorthodox move.

On 25 January Hugh set off with Vanessa and his second secretary Alp Mehmet in the ambassadorial black Jaguar. Arriving at his hotel, he was unable to reach Doina Cornea on the telephone. He wanted to give her the option of refusing to see him, so he wrote out a note to give to her.

We saw there was a policeman outside the fence in front of a small garden... Doina Cornea and her husband came out of the front door into the garden...I explained why we had come and she told the policeman that she was willing to receive my note and me. Alp Mehmet then took the note from me and threw it over the fence. The policeman ran through the gate, picked up the note and put it in his pocket before coming out again and facing up to me. Doina was in the meantime saying this was appalling, an abuse of her rights and that we should tell everyone in Vienna (where the CSCE conference was in its last stages) while Vanessa tried without success in the mêlée to put a film in her camera.... The policeman used physical force to prevent us getting near to Doina. He seemed to be nervous, as we were, although beginning to get angry...Before we gave up and left, Vanessa had been able to hold Doina Cornea's hand and tell her how much we admired her for what she was doing.

Back at the hotel, Hugh Arbuthnott telephoned his deputy in Bucharest, asking him to report to the Foreign Office what had happened and to call on the Romanian authorities to protest about the way he had been treated. Meanwhile he continued his prearranged schedule with a visit to the Cluj Village Museum and a call on the Catholic bishop. In the evening he and Vanessa met up with a Romanian couple at the theatre to see *My Fair Lady* (in Romanian) before giving a big dinner to local dignitaries. The couple

were pleasant enough and seemed to enjoy the show as we did (up to a point). During the performance, someone came into our box and whispered to them. At the first interval they made their excuses and left, saying they had a family problem and would not be able to join us for dinner in our hotel. Back there a huge meal was laid out for fifteen people or so but we had to eat what we could on our own. Our guests had obviously been warned off and not a single person turned up.

Within hours news of the Arbuthnotts' aborted meeting with Cornea was broadcast on the BBC Romanian Service and Radio Free Europe. Hugh's foray had the support of the Foreign Office but the diplomatic corps in Bucharest was generally unsympathetic. The French ambassador thought that Hugh should have followed his own example by asking permission from the Ministry of Foreign Affairs for permission to visit Cornea – such formalities must, it seemed, be upheld to the bitter end. But when ordinary Romanians were able to speak to Hugh, they told him of their profound gratitude that someone of his rank had at last given Cornea open encouragement. More and more, she was seen as *the* embodiment of resistance.

On 8 March 1989 the European Community lodged a protest about Cornea's harassment and on the same day the Conference of Communities and Regions of Europe adopted a resolution recommending support for the threatened Romanian villages. An avalanche of criticism now descended on Ceaușescu, with the UN Human Rights Commission and the International Federation of Free Trade Unions belatedly joining the chorus. On 10 March three aged former members of the Politburo and other ancient Party veterans, including Brucan, released to the BBC an open letter to Ceaușescu. By contrast with Cornea's wonderful letters, the text, which argued for continued allegiance to the one-party state, seemed from another world. 'The very idea of socialism for which we have fought', they wrote, 'is discredited by [Ceaușescu's] policy.'

Our friends in Bucharest remained defiant. On 13 March Dinescu wrote a letter of denunciation to the President of the Writers' Union; Pleşu and the magazine editor, Dan Haulica, followed with letters of support. All three were put under house arrest. A month later, after the BBC had broadcast two more letters from Doina Cornea, she was attacked in the street. Just when Hugh Arbuthnott was needed most, his term as ambassador was up. Cornea managed to get word to the British Embassy about how much she had appreciated his farewell telegram, of which she had heard through the BBC World Service.

Prince Charles at last found the occasion to speak about Romania on 27 April. While opening an exhibition at the Civic Trust, he treated an unsuspecting audience to a powerful invective on the destruction of Romania's heritage, ending with a long quote from Doina Cornea's letter that Mark had smuggled from Cluj. The speech made headlines all over Europe. But he had not found it easy and wrote to me afterwards:

I find I have a terrible knotted feeling in the pit of my tummy as the courage is plucked up from somewhere deep inside... Having made the speech I then usually have second thoughts and feel I shouldn't have done it and it would be so much easier to lead a quieter life! But there is something, somewhere, telling one that I can't do that and that I wouldn't be true to myself if I did stay quiet instead of taking the risk and accepting the challenge...Anyway I hope what I said helps to stir up the debate and raise some people's awareness. I also hope you receive this before some frightful undercover agent stabs me in the left buttock with a poisoned umbrella!
PS I hope Charlie would approve of our efforts...?

The penultimate remark in Prince Charles's letter referred to the death of the dissident Bulgarian émigré Georgi Markov, assassinated in broad daylight on Waterloo Bridge by a Communist agent carrying a phial of poison in the pointed tip of an umbrella. Although we joked about such things at the Eminescu meetings, and pretended not to take the risk seriously, the truth was that the murder of so many Romanian émigrés caused us all a nagging anxiety. In retrospect, I do not feel I was being overdramatic in leaving specific instructions that any 'accident' that happened to me should be treated as suspicious.

The Civic Trust now agreed to lend us a room in Carlton House Terrace, which helped us to put our campaign for the Romanian villages on a more professional footing. We promptly joined forces with the Brussels-based Opération Villages Roumains, run by two Belgians who had put the full list of 13,000 Romanian villages on a database and had launched an imaginative twinning and adoption programme. The response was not always positive. In my own village I failed dismally. The chairman of the Quenington Parish Council refused to put the request to twin with Sângiorgiu de Pădure on the agenda at the quarterly meeting, explaining that she did not want Quenington 'involved in that sort of thing'. But one of our London committee members, Mary Walsh, who lived in Herefordshire, was first off the mark when her village adopted Gârbău near Cluj. Soon after, her neighbours in Vowchurch took on Inlaceni – a village close to the tomb of Prince Charles's female ancestor.

How strange it now seems that even at this terminal stage, when all was disintegrating around him, none of us could conceive that Ceauşescu would ever really go or that the Soviet empire would actually collapse. As the net of misery and destruction closed in, we knew it to be more important than ever to keep contact with our friends in Romania. There was clearly, however, no point in my trying to go back. In the extremely unlikely event of my getting a visa no one would risk coming to see my paintings at the gallery. Moreover, despite a letter from the Union of Fine Arts making tentative proposals about the event, I knew that the authorities had no intention of letting the exhibition take place, which was corroborated when I subsequently read the secret police files.

Even our low-profile volunteers met with difficulties, for by this time the Securitate had our measure. We were either tracked in England or our messengers were uncovered when they arrived in Bucharest. I do not know which. David Westover, a councillor in Hammersmith, was roughly interviewed by the Securitate after three days: 'Tell Mrs Jessica Douglas-Home and Mr Mark Almond that they should refrain from sending their men to Romania.' In the late spring James de Candole, a young philosophy student at London University, was ordered to leave the country within twenty-four hours because of 'activities hostile to the state'. At the end of the interrogation they told him: 'Inform your controller in London to stop this unfriendly activity.'

Then we had a breakthrough. John Laughland, who was half Romanian and fluent in the language, succeeded in reaching the northern part of the country via Hungary, and spent four untroubled weeks in Romania in July and August. Probably it was helpful that he had taken the unusual step early in his stay of having dinner with a friendly Securitate agent, who worked in the Cluj tourist office and seemed satisfied with the explanation of a family connection as being the reason for his interest in the country.

John had taken in his suitcase twenty or so expensive books, bought at Blackwell's with Eminescu Trust money, nearly all of which went undiscovered at the Hungarian border. (The exceptions were King Carol's autobiography and a book on *perestroika*, both of which he was openly reading on the train and were duly confiscated) He also brought with him free *Spectator* subscription forms for a number of contacts, including a new one, Stelian Tănase, who was said to be starting a magazine.

Tănase turned out to be another Romanian mystery that we were never quite to fathom. In his thirties, with a flowing beard, he enjoyed striking poses. In peculiarly free and easy conversation with us, conducted with histrionic panache, he told us that his every move was under scrutiny. Yet he never seemed to have any real trouble with the police. Despite our cynicism, John Laughland remained serenely convinced about Stelian Tănase's *bona fides*:

The main project now [his report said] is Stelian's proposed political novel, which he hopes to publish in England. I must get down to alerting publishers...If we could help him with this it would be a real coup, since he is that rare thing in Romania, a <u>genuine</u> dissident! He wants to publish articles and give interviews and all the razzmatazz. I imagine the *Spectator* would be fairly keen on the articles...the other thing with him is that he wants to come to London and Paris during March of next year and needs money....I would be very keen to manage his visit.

In Bucharest, John found Gabriel Liiceanu depressed. He had been refused a visa to the Heidegger conference in Germany, and his public protest had added another black mark in his file. He was tormented by indecision. Should he sacrifice himself like Andrei Pleşu? Or should he limit himself to trying to preserve some kind of Romanian culture for future generations? His conscience and temperament often told him to take the riskier path, but he believed that in the final analysis he could do more good by pure philosophy. Once so close, Pleşu and Liiceanu now found themselves on different tacks. Pleşu was immersing himself in Lenin, equipping himself to argue from strength about the mainsprings of Communism, while Liiceanu was translating Derrida, the fashionable French purveyor of 'deconstruction'.

John went to see Mariana Celac.

Normally, her house is under supervision [he wrote], but as she works they generally do not have anybody guarding the door during the day. Fortunately I arrived before she got back from work, when there was no policeman at the door. Her mother let me in and Mariana returned about 5 pm. She is often followed in a deliberately intimidating way when she goes around town, and clearly suffers under this. She emphasises the splitting of the opposition ... contact among her friends is fairly minimal; she points out that the opposition has not even got to the stage of undertaking any action: its only crime so far has been to express an opinion, and for this people are clamped down on immediately.

On the last day of John's stay Andrei Pippidi risked dining with him in public in the restaurant of the Athéné Palace Hotel, where over a bottle of wine, echoing Mariana Celac's thoughts, Pippidi voiced his dismay at the splitting of Romanian society. Even during the terror of the 1950s he had found it relatively easy to live in hiding for a year, sheltering with friends or friends of friends. Today such unselfish courage on behalf of others would be unthinkable. As for getting rid of Ceauşescu, isolated acts of protest against the regime could never grow into an uprising. The only hope lay in an accident, some unforeseen external event.

Just as our friends' morale was at its lowest, the end was approaching. The borders between East Germany, Hungary and Austria were cracking and a torrent of refugees was on the move. Our last emissary was Dr Anthony Daniels (known to readers of the *Spectator* as Dr Theodore Dalrymple) who worked as a psychiatrist in a Birmingham prison. In *The Wilder Shores of Marx*, written immediately after Ceauşescu's downfall two months later, he published a vivid account of his mission, as did our first visitor, David Selbourne, in *Death of a Hero*.

During his two-week visit at the end of September, Anthony Daniels travelled approximately 1,500 miles throughout the country.

I did not visit Mariana Celac because the British Embassy informed me that she had requested 6 weeks previously that no foreigner should visit her until further notice ...In spite of others' doubts about him my intuition about Mr Stelian Tănase is that he is highly egotistic and rather enjoys the role of dissident, making himself somewhat conspicuous by blacking out his windows. These precautions, it seemed to me, were more likely to draw the attention of the police to him than the reverse...was he dramatising his position in order to impress me, a person of limited experience? He had a strange intensity about him, a burning quality. I wondered whether he thought of himself as the Solzhenitsyn of Romania. Was it real, this similarity, or assumed? Everything he did was on a grand scale; giving me food, bread and cheese, he cut hunks with the passion of Goya's Satan devouring his own children. He was writing a novel in the style of Gogol (realism was insufficient to capture the madness of Romania, he said)... He would like some Hume – I would suggest the *Enquiries*, the *Essays* and the *Dialogues Concerning Natural Religion*.

Various people suggested to me that he was an *agent provocateur* and warned me to be wary of him. I felt out of my depth, or as though I had, like Alice, stepped through the looking glass and entered a world where everything was familiar yet changed, where nothing was what it appeared to be, where ignorance was guilt and trust foolishness.

Travelling eastwards to Braşov, Anthony Daniels took some books to the youngest of our contacts, Claudiu Secaşiu, a historian in his twenties who was researching the pre-First World War politicians and had a daytime job in the local museum. We knew that the Securitate had once tried to recruit Secaşiu. Daniels reported that they had had a second try, but had left him alone when he refused. His museum had been asked to prepare a list of villages in the region, stating their historical importance, to enable the authorities to determine which were most suitable for destruction. 'I delivered all the books. I also took a few medicines – especially eye drops – and chocolate truffles (though I ate one myself – and then felt very guilty about it – when the meal in the hotel was just too disgusting)...'

Operation Romanian Villages was eating up money, so I decided to hold another fund-raising event in the country. It took place on a gloomy November evening. I had designed a poster of Romanian dancing girls, which I pinned up on telegraph poles and notice boards in nearby villages. Stalls were set up inside the mill room, where five years earlier Zenga Long-more had sung her pre-war Blues for the Czechs. Pony rides were on offer until dark at 5.30 and Diana Phipps had reluctantly agreed to tell fortunes again. Outside the French windows we erected a rough canvas tent, borrowed from the local army unit. Here tiny Lucy Swainson, a village friend living just up the hill in Quenington, who ran the smallest pub in England, kept her beer and soft-drink stall for four cold windy hours, in gloves and woollen hat, her long scarf criss-crossing her head. This was not what I had hoped for when I had planned the fête on a warm September afternoon, but the sombre weather seemed appropriate for poor Romania.

At the back of the mill room, up a ladder to a cramped minstrels' gallery, I had arranged for four Romanian émigrés to sing native folksong. I should have explained to them at the outset that they were not to be the star turns, only to provide evocative background music. Or perhaps I should have been more sympathetic to their sensitivities. One by one each singer came to me to complain. They were too cold; they could not climb the sheer wall ladder to the gallery; they were not treated with enough respect; they must insist on silence while they sang. My patience nearly broke when they refused to travel back with Christian Mititelu (who had brought them to Gloucestershire in his car), on the whispered grounds that he was a Communist agent. Luckily I had my own collection of Romanian songs on tape. To cover up the carping hullabaloo, I kept the tape-recorder on at full blast.

I was beginning to despair of Diana Phipps when she suddenly appeared at 6.30 through the French windows, bringing with her a dark-haired, enigmatic young woman. 'This is Rose. You must use her. She has the real talent.' I threw the mysterious girl into the small sitting room at the back of the house, placing her by a large log fire. As she prepared her props on a stool and assembled her cards, a queue quickly formed down the passage, responding to the atavistic allure of the witch's profession. Diana had picked up Rose in London, near

Notting Hill Gate. She appeared to be a real gypsy. The first person who went into her den remained a good twenty minutes before rattling open the sitting room door, rushing down the passage and out of the house back to London. A quarter of an hour later another white-faced figure came out, shattered not by Rose's prognostications for the future but by her uncanny perceptions of the past. My own tarot reading told of a job I would get from an older man, which would involve much travel. Two months later George Soros offered me work for his foundation in Romania.

The real star of the fête, however, was 'Denis Thatcher'. Several years previously I had designed the costumes for John Wells's play *Anyone for Denis?* – a farce about the Thatchers' home life. Even though I was fond of the Prime Minister's husband, I found nothing unkind in Wells's impersonation of him as a gin-swilling golf club fogey, for he was portrayed with humanity and genuine affection. 'Tincture' in hand, Wells cajoled the crowd for a good half hour to give to the cause. As he warned against the presence of 'pinkos' in our midst, the émigrés exchanged knowing looks or uneasy glances – some of them seemed far from sure whether 'Denis' was the real thing or an improvisation.

As the evening came to an end, I wandered out to see how Lucy Swainson was getting on in the tent, where to dispel the frost we had installed an industrial electric blower. Near the stables by the river, I found David Selbourne in the dark crouched in the front seat of his car, listening to the BBC. 'Zhivkov is gone. Mass demonstrations in Sofia,' he hissed at me. I stared in disbelief. Surrounded by a collapsing Eastern bloc – Poland, Hungary, East Germany, Czechoslovakia and now Bulgaria – this surely meant meltdown for Romania. Ceauşescu must be next to go.

Epilogue

Many call themselves dissidents nowadays. But a dissident was someone who was prepared to put their name to their words. You who came from England – my mother and I had code names for you. We called Noel Malcolm 'the Romanian'. He looked like us. He came when he was very ill. You, we called *angelotto*. But Mark Almond – oh my goodness. His height. His fair, red hair. His gold spectacles and his long, long black coat. We called him after a character in Dickens. Together, you made it possible for me to continue doing what I did – to survive. Not in the way you might think, through telling the world about us. It was more that for a short time – after the knock on the door, the sight of one of your faces through the crack – my solitary life became less hard to bear. I felt no longer alone.

Mariana Celac, talking over coffee at the RIBA
during a visit to London in 1997

F ive days after the fête, a neighbour rushed through my front door to tell me that he had found Tara lying in the road a mile from the village, his car crushed by a collision with a bus. I raced to the scene. By a miracle a woman who had just completed a first aid survival course had come across the accident. She saved Tara from asphyxiation by keeping his lungs free from blood until the ambulance arrived. He had terrible injuries, but was operated on with great skill at Princess Margaret Hospital in Swindon, and within two months was well on his way to recovery.

My daily drives to and from the hospital were punctuated by exhilarating news bulletins about events in Romania. But when I watched the television clips at home, the dramatic sequence of developments before and after Ceauşescu's execution appeared to me stage-managed: his 'trial', the take-over of the television studios, the Securitate's 'battles to restore order' in the towns, the patently exaggerated (and rapidly refuted) accounts of the numbers of deaths, Iliescu's unexplained rise to power and the mysterious 'emergence' of his National Salvation Front. None of these had the air of spontaneity. That Iliescu had old and close Moscow connections was widely known, but the extent of the Soviet role at the time of Ceauşescu's death remains a secret to this day.

The circumstances of our friends were, of course, transformed by the ending of the Cold War. Andrei Pleşu became Minister of Culture (in 1998 he was made Foreign Minister), while Gabriel Liiceanu took over the State publishing house, privatised it and renamed it Humanitas. In Czechoslovakia Havel, Bratinka, Benda, Čarnogorský and Alena Hromádková would all attain high office.

Late in January, in an old palace in Prague off Wenceslas Square, Czechs and Slovaks convened for the first time in open discussion with Western academics and politicians. To say that this was the culmination of all that we had been working for would make a model ending to my story. But it was not. Bratinka spoke of the Slovak problem, and of the Sudeten Germans. Benda warned that totalitarianism was not dead: democracy would not fall into place simply by holding free elections. Alena, on the eve of founding her own party, was vehement about the need to address the past. Wise and prescient words were spoken. But the mood was one of feeling the way forwards, sensing the burden of the long haul ahead, stumbling into the light, like the prisoners in *Fidelio*.

It was somewhat symptomatic of the opposition that we had so often encountered at home that the only journalist to cover the conference was Richard Gott of the *Guardian*. Under the headline 'Blue Pimpernels' he sneered at the dissidents' clothes, ridiculed their conservative politics and made a travesty of the proceedings. In 1996 it was revealed that he had for years been in the pay of the Soviets.

One morning in April 1990 an envelope dropped on my doormat covered in Romanian stamps. It was from Victor Grădinariu. We had had no contact since our farewell on the darkened platform of Bucharest's Gǎra de Nord several years previously.

It took a long time before I finally made up my mind to bother you with this letter [he began without addressing me by name]. Olivia Manning's *Balkan Trilogy*, the book you've kindly offered me in 1987 when we both travelled to Bucharest in the same train, is now a record of a too short glimpse out to the free world. To that free world that we here couldn't dream of in those dark years. And the memory of that unexpected event has finally succeeded to make me send this letter.

As you may have noticed, a Revolution has been performed last December in our country. Unfortunately I am no hero of that Revolution because there has been no riots in Iaşi – nevertheless the fact is that the uprising was intended to begin on the 14th December, but the forces of the oppression have developed large scale discouraging actions and finally fear won and nothing happened.

Three years ago you have told me to continue the fight. Now the fight is by no means completed, on the contrary everything is yet to be done to reach real freedom and democracy. I should be very happy to see you again and continue our talk – there are so many things to tell – but Big Brother's eyes are not yet blue and I send you this letter from inside.

I am convinced that after visiting our country, you have already endorsed our struggle; I believe in you and in what you have already done for us and I'm still counting on you for a few aspects concerning our present situation: our problem is that now we need even more help than before ...

Coming quite unexpectedly from a stranger with whom I had formed only a fleeting friendship, the letter had a powerful and lasting effect. By coincidence, the next day a call came asking me to join an international delegation being organised in Washington to observe the following month's Romanian elections – the first free elections since the war. Although I was busy designing the costumes for a production of the *Mikado*, after Victor's letter I could not refuse. I was to cover the voting stations to the north of Iaşi. Victor would be my guide and interpreter.

Victor had scarcely changed and was as full of energy as ever. Dispensing with breakfast, we rose early to cover the area along the Moldavian border. The sky was blue, the countryside alight with sun. Every village had a carnival atmosphere. There were farmers in their best suits, children with the day off from school, women in flowered shawls and scarves pressing wild irises into our hands, tables laid out with cake and orange juice. At midday we drove to the painted churches. In the hills and fields behind Voroneţ and Suceviţa men carried mobile voting boxes for the shepherds, made of cardboard with rough slits for the ballot papers. There was a mood of undreamed of hope and excitement, even if in our stretch of 200 miles we saw barely one polling station with secure election procedures.

The count was held up for a suspiciously long time. It was a good four days before Iliescu's victory was announced in Bucharest. The British cross-party parliamentary delegation immediately held a press conference at Westminster. Pronouncing the elections free and fair, its spokeswoman, Edwina Curry, said that the British observers were 'thrilled' by what they had experienced. I challenged this verdict. Our team had found the process deeply flawed. Throughout the campaign the media had been controlled by the National Salvation Front and the opposition's voice had been stifled. Almost all the mayors in the towns and villages had been unreformed Ceauşescu appointees – it was they who had administered the polling booths and provided 'friendly advice' to the bewildered voters.

My intervention achieved nothing. Nor did Noel Malcolm's and Mark Almond's articles in the *Spectator* and *The Times*.

The majority of the Western media endorsed the election results. Victor was in despair. He wrote again:

> Well, it's all over now. The campaign and the elections are now history, but our future was born on the 20th May and the way time has begun to flow then does nothing but consternate us... personally I don't think that fraud exceeded 20% of the final results and that is the most depressing thing. So many people have died last December, so many have tried their best during the unfair fight of the last five months; they all believed that Communism would be banished in Romania. And finally we succeeded in being the only nation on earth which has restored Communism by its own free will.
>
> All the structures of the past are untouched and the few gaps that have accidentally occurred are, or will be filled soon with new brave Communists that are so eager to prove their best. Discrediting intellectuals and dissidents is considered as an important duty for the Communist press. The general feeling is that of tiredness and resignation. Many people seem to regret their vote already and they used to say that 'things can't get worse than before'. I think everything is already bad enough but the fact is that we have missed our train and there won't be another one until the next elections, in two years. So the matter is how to act efficiently during these two years in order to avoid that another 20th May disaster ever happens again.

If only the Romanians had been offered a way to come to terms with Ceauşescu's legacy, Victor's fearful premonitions might not have been realised. In 1991 the Czechs passed a 'cleansing law', temporarily banning police agents and collaborators from certain posts. But the saga of Romania's secret police files is a running sore to this day. During the uprising of December 1989 thousands of dossiers went up in flames in Sibiu when the Army fired on the Securitate building. Many more were destroyed later. In 1993 the remains of a massive bonfire of papers were discovered just north of Bucharest.

Soon after Ceauşescu's death, the dissidents tried unsuccessfully to get control of the remaining files. Their every attempt was blocked by the sinister plotter Virgil Măgureanu, the head of the Romanian 'Information Service' as the Securitate were now renamed. (Once Ceauşescu's expert on the West, Măgureanu had presided over his master's execution in the army barracks at Tirgoviste in December 1989.) Most Romanians regarded with blank incredulity Măgureanu's claim to have revamped the secret police and disposed of its telephone tapping equipment. In a belated and unconvincing stab at transparency, he finally arranged to lift selected extracts from the Securitate dossiers for publication in the *Cartea Alba*, the White Book.

When Claudiu Secaşiu called me in April 1997 to tell me that there were references to me in the *Cartea Alba*, he agreed to help me gain access to the original files. This would require a direct order from Măgureanu. To fraternise with him on his home territory felt like a betrayal of all those he had spied on, ruined or assassinated over the years. Nevertheless, when the invitation came to have tea with him at the old Securitate headquarters, I accepted.

I arrived with Secaşiu at an anonymous gateway half way to Otopeni airport. I had passed this fenced-off, top secret security zone in no man's land every time I had landed in Romania. Once my driver had gesticulated agitatedly towards the wire railings, muttering that it was there that Ceauşescu's most evil operations were hatched. Now we were waved through the police check and drove over acres of flat concrete to a massive 1950s building. In the front drive soldiers were hoeing rose beds, pretending to be engrossed in their work.

A figure appeared by the car. 'Would Doamna Jessica come this way?' Ahead, Măgureanu's deputy and his translator were waiting for us on the steps. On entering the hall, through shafts of light magnified by huge windows, I was confronted by the squat silhouette of Măgureanu.

'The sun is shining – brighter – every – yes, every day' he said in Romanian, giving me a long penetrating look.

'Yes,' I replied, 'the King has arrived in Romania.'

This was not what Măgureanu wanted to hear. 'The two are not connected,' he rejoined coldly.

We climbed the staircase to a huge room decorated in 1950s furniture, with ugly chairs covered by shining pink and pale-mauve patterned satin. He pointed to his collection of Romanian contemporary art on the walls before gesturing me to sit facing him at a small round table. He stared at me with dead, almond-coloured little eyes. I wondered if he was practising some Securitate technique of mesmerism.

'So you have come to see me in Romania. I always knew you would.'

My discomfort grew.

'It gives me great pleasure to meet you in this place,' Măgureanu went on.

I had to wrest myself from that stare. I looked left to the interpreter. I saw my way out. I would address my remarks only to him.

Măgureanu's reason for agreeing to see me soon became clear. Romania's application for NATO membership had been damaged by a recent diplomatic incident. The British held the Romanian Information Service responsible for a break-in at one of their Bucharest embassy residences. The amateurish Securitate intruders had left tell-tale cigarette stubs in the ashtrays.

'I have been blackened by the British Foreign Office and the Americans,' Măgureanu said. 'I am the innocent victim of KGB disinformation. Their agents have planted incriminating evidence against my Information Service.'

For a quarter of an hour I listened to his monologue, then I interrupted him. 'Can I see my files?'

'Yes, provided you do not tell others you have done so. The law for Romanians to see their own files is not yet in place.' Now he had done with me. 'Goodbye – I intend to dedicate myself to helping my country.' Long pause. 'To go perhaps into politics – my career is nearly over.' Another long pause. 'I will help the younger generation, like Mr Secaşiu here, to enter politics.'

Next day Secaşiu called the warehouse, a routine he had performed daily for three weeks. But it was not until the day of my departure that Măgureanu finished his cat-and-mouse game. Word came that the files had been 'found'. We were to arrive at exactly 11 am.

We set out in good time, travelling by tram five kilometres into Bucharest's military zone. Across a rubble courtyard through a grey steel gate guarded by soldiers, we entered a vast concrete warehouse. We were led into a little side room and introduced to the editor of the *Cartea Alba*. He was immediately on the defensive 'We have been much criticised for being subjective. But all selection is subjective,' he said. 'I have chosen our text for the especially good details it conveys.'

Boxes were brought in and manuscripts, bound with brown string, were opened in front of us, revealing cream-coloured tissue-paper pages of sharply indented, plumply rounded typewritten lettering. Were these recently concocted fakes? Had they been tampered with? I thought not.

Why, I asked, was the typescript so large and thick compared to an ordinary typewriter?

'For efficiency. For the specialists to read quickly without glasses.'

The agent delegated to spy on us in the 1980s had signed his name clearly in strong black ink at the end of each report. This was followed by 'I submit for information the present notes' with a counter-signature from Tudor Postelnicu, Ceauşescu's Minister of the Interior. The layout had a startling aesthetic intensity. As I turned to the beginning and began reading – with Secaşiu's help – I was shocked and exhilarated. It was as though I was watching a secret film of an earlier part of my life taken by a deadly enemy. For five hours or more we read and took notes. Then, as abruptly as we had been admitted, the session was terminated.

In December 1999 the Romanian Parliament finally voted to set up a committee to oversee the release and curatorship of the Securitate archives. No money, however, has yet been forthcoming, either for the absurdly inadequate proposed staff or for a suitable place to house the mountains of documents. Perhaps, too, the will to know the truth is lacking. Some need no persuading of the all-pervading fear and daily betrayals of those times. But the world at large is indifferent. It remains as fascinated as ever by the crimes of the Nazis. But it is already forgetting the equally horrific, and far more extensive, criminality of Communism. Those who were silent have forgiven themselves, while those who risked everything to fight against it are regarded less as heroes than as an embarrassment.

How has this twisting of history come about? Certainly, the Soviets were past masters at exploiting the language of idealism. Even so, it is hard to understand how so many in the West were taken in. The dissidents saw the corruption of the meaning of words with wonderful clarity and found the courage to resist the suppression that sustained it. Yet who can say how enduring a legacy they have left to the generation that succeeds them? The forces that have swept across Eastern Europe since the fall of the Berlin Wall are also sweeping away many of the values for which the dissidents suffered. Far from re-connecting to their past, the people find themselves dragged into the seedy back-streets of mafioso capitalism, where all too often they encounter their old oppressors re-invented as 'businessmen'. If they have hopes for the future, it is more as provincial inhabitants of a bureaucratic European Union than as proud inheritors of the traditions and achievements of the country where they were raised.

Mine was a strange adventure – a journey into parts of the collective memory of Central Europe. Will that collective memory survive? Or will that, too, gather dust in a neglected archive?

Biographical Notes

Václav Benda (1946–99)

A philosopher who, after losing his position at the Charles University in 1970 and signing Charter 77, was forced to work as a stoker. Imprisoned 1979–83 as a member of the Committee for the Defence of the Unjustly Prosecuted (VONS). Active in *samizdat* and other independent activities. In 1990 founded the Christian Democrat Party (KDS) and was elected to Parliament. At the time of his death was serving as a Senator in the upper house.

Pavel Bratinka (b. 1946)

A nuclear physicist who, after 1981, was forced to work as cleaner in the Metro and a stoker. Author of *samizdat* works and active in the independent culture. In 1990 founded the Civic Democratic Alliance (ODA) and entered Parliament, becoming Deputy Foreign Minister and from 1996–7 Minister without Portfolio. Now Managing Director of Euroffice and Vice-President of the Prague Society for International Cooperation.

Ján Čarnogorský (b. 1944)

A lawyer struck off the register in 1981 for defending a Charter 77 signatory, leader of an underground seminar and producer of *samizdat*. Active in the underground Church and underground politics, imprisoned Sept.–Nov. 1989. Following his release, helped to establish Public Against Violence in Bratislava and later founded the Slovak Christian Democrat Party. Became Deputy Prime Minister of Czechoslovakia in 1990, later Slovak Prime Minister; is now (2000) Minister of Justice in Slovakia.

Václav Havel (b. 1936)

Prevented by his 'bourgeois' background from receiving a university education, in the 1960s a successful playwright and intellectual leader, in 1976 one of the creators and first spokesmen of Charter 77. Imprisoned several times on human rights issues, was elected President of Czechoslovakia after the velvet revolution, and subsequently President of the Czech Republic.

Ladislav Hejdánek (b. 1927)
A philosopher who for more than thirty years following his graduation in 1952 was forced to accept menial employment. One of the earliest leaders of the home seminars; his open seminar every Monday evening was the venue for lectures by scores of internationally-known academics. After 1989 he became Professor of Philosophy at the protestant Faculty of Theology of the Charles University.

Karel Hubka
One of the most talented students attending Petr Rezek's home seminars in philosophy in the 1980s. Married to the historian of classical theatre, Eva Stehlíková. A specialist in computer science, he reached Britain in 1984 on an invitation from the Institute of Classical Studies. Having decided not to return to Czechoslovakia, he committed suicide in London in 1986.

Alena Hromádková (b. 1943)
Father was a lawyer forbidden to practise by the Communists. Her forte in the 'dissident' society was as a networker, particularly in briefing English-speaking visitors on the situation under Communism. After 1989 she founded the Democratic Union Party, which she led for several years; the party is today (2000) one of the Coalition of Four.

Jan Kavan (b. 1946)
Born in England, the son of a firmly Communist British-Czech marriage. On return to Czechoslovakia, Kavan's father was sentenced to prison in one of the 1950s Prague show trials. After the Soviet invasion of 1968, Kavan (who had been involved in the student movement) spent twenty years in London, organising support movements for the dissidents in Czechoslovakia. In the early 1990s he was accused of having worked for the secret police and suffered two heart

attacks, but in 1998 he became Foreign Minister in the Social Democrat government; in 1999 deputy Prime Minister.

Rudolf Kučera (b. 1947)
A political scientist with a particular interest in the lands of former Austro-Hungary and the pan-European movement. During the 1980s he led an underground seminar group on Central Europe and founded a journal of the same name, of which he is still editor. After 1989 he became head of the Political Science Institute of the Faculty of Social Sciences of the Charles University, and is a regular commentator on current events.

Broňa Müllerová
The daughter of Czechs active in opposition to the totalitarian regime, both imprisoned for number of years by the Communists. She is married to the underground activist Jiří Müller, with whom she worked on many *samizdat* projects in Brno during the 1980s. She is a professional translator from Czech to English and mother of two children.

Jiří Müller (b. 1943)
An important student leader during the Prague Spring of 1968. Imprisoned 1971–6 for distributing leaflets informing the general public of their right not to vote in the general election. Following this he worked on a multitude of projects aimed at bridging the gap between the 'dissident ghetto' and the general public. Described by the secret police as 'one of the ten most dangerous men in Moravia'. After 1989 he was appointed by Václav Havel to cleanse the secret police, but subsequently avoided high-profile roles, preferring to act in an advisory capacity.

Eva Oslzlá
One of the fortunate students who had an opportunity to study in the 'window of opportunity' at the end of the 1960s. Although graduating in French, she was subsequently forbidden to teach Czech students. She worked with her husband Petr Oslzlý in establishing the most important underground seminar in Brno and was active in the independent culture. After 1989 she requalified as a teacher of French.

Karel Palek (b. 1946)
Graduated in philology at the end of the 1960s, but rather than take an academic post he preferred to work in a boilerhouse where he wrote and edited *samizdat* under the pseudonyms Petr Fidelius and Pius. Founder the journal *Kritický sborník,* which he still edits; one of his *samizdat* works was published in France as *L'esprit post-totalitaire* (1983).

Radim Palouš (b. 1924)
Pupil of the philosopher Jan Patočka, after 1968 co-organiser of an underground seminar based on the works of Patočka and other philosophers. Signatory and (in 1982–3) a spokesman of Charter 77; in 1990 appointed the first post-Communist Rector of the Charles University.

Jan Patočka (1907–77)
Studied philosophy in Prague and Paris between the wars, being influenced by Husserl and Heidegger. Forced to work as a labourer during the war, he taught intensively at the Charles University in the immediate post-war period but was marginalised under the Communists. Allowed back to the university for a brief period at the end of the 1960s, he continued to teach at underground seminars in the 1970s. He became one of the first three spokesmen of Charter 77, but after intense police interrogation died of a stroke. His works have been archived and published by his students.

Petr Pithart (b. 1941)
A lawyer and historian who, after a Communist youth, spent the 1970s and 1980s active in the sphere of independent culture and learning. Following Václav Havel's election as President of Czechoslovakia, he became leader of Civic Forum and subsequently Czech Prime Minister. He was later elected a senator, and for a period leader of the Senate.

Miroslav Pospíšil (b. 1951)
Graduated from the Masaryk University as the best student in English in his year, but after refusing to join the Communist Party was forbidden to teach at the university. He spent many years as teacher at the State Language School, during which time he also became co-

organiser of the leading underground seminar in Brno and joined in many other independent projects. In 1990 he established the Czechoslovak Jan Hus Educational Foundation as an official organisation, and directed it for more than ten years.

Petr Rezek (b. 1948)
A student of Jan Patočka and a key partner in university-level philosophy courses organised by the Jan Hus Foundation in the 1980s. Considered to be one of the best Czech philosophers, he was appointed to the Charles University in 1990 and expected to become head of the philosophy department, but resigned after some difficult conflicts with his colleagues. He is now the publisher of high-quality editions of philosophical works.

Karel Srp (b. 1937)
During the 1970s and 1980s led the Jazz Section of the Musicians' Union, and succeeded in making it virtually autonomous of Communist control. The Jazz Section organised events for young people and published literature otherwise unavailable in Czechoslovakia. After some years of persecution he and other members were imprisoned in an internationally-publicised trial (1986). After 1989 he led the organisation Artforum, but fell under the shadow of accusations of having worked with the secret police.

Cardinal František Tomášek (1899–1992)
In the 1950s spent several years in a Czech labour camp. He then spent several years in charge of a small parish although, on orders of the Pope, he had secretly been ordained bishop. When Cardinal Beran was forced into exile, Tomášek was appointed to Prague and in 1977 made Cardinal. He increasingly spoke out against the Communist suppression of human rights, and on 25 November 1989 publicly supported the velvet revolution. He helped to organise the visit to Prague of Pope John Paul II in 1990, and resigned for reasons of age in 1991.

Alex Tomsky (b. 1947)
Political scientist who left Czechoslovakia after the Russian invasion of 1968 and studied at the London School of Economics. Founder of the journal and publishing house *Rozmluvy* which specialised in

small-format editions of Czech and world literature which could be smuggled into Czechoslovakia. He also worked with the underground Church. After 1989 returned to Czechoslovakia and became head of Academia, publishing house of the Academy of Sciences of the Czech Republic.

ROMANIA

Mihai Botez (1940–96)

Mathematician, scientific researcher and professor at Bucharest University. Former member of Romanian Communist Party, he tried to influence Ceauşescu's economic policy. Because of published criticisms of the regime, he lost all positions in 1977. Banished to teaching in the provinces (Tulcea). In 1987 he was allowed to leave for USA, where he sought political asylum. After 1990 he became Romanias Ambassador at UN. Published articles and books of political analysis.

Mariana Celac (b. 1936)

Architect. After her husband left for USA, she became a strong critic of Ceauşescu's architectural planning policy. In 1988 she was demoted within her architectural institute after an interview with the French newspaper *Libération*. Immediately after Ceauşescu's fall, she became a founder member of the Group for Social Dialogue, an intellectual talking-shop populated by former dissidents and which established itself in Nicu Ceauşescu's palace in Calea Victoreie. Writes for literary and cultural journals.

Mircea Dinescu (b. 1950)

Poet. Member of Communist Party. Dissident. Published several volumes of poetry before 1990 (one in Britain). He was placed under house arrest between 1988 and 1989, partly as a result of an interview given to the same French newspaper as Mariana Celac, partly for his attempts to write an open critical letter from the Writers' Union. One of the few who reached the Bucharest television studios during the civil war which followed Ceauşescu's escape from the city in December 1989. Founder member of the Council of the National Salvation Front. After 1990 he continued to write verse and essays.

Published in Germany, Holland, France, Britain and Sweden. President of Writers' Union 1990–94.

Ion Ilici Iliescu (b. 1930)
Son of a Communist railway worker, he joined the Communist Youth Union at 14. Trained as a hydroelectric power engineer in Bucharest and Moscow (where he served as leader of the Romanian students resident in the Soviet Union). As Chairman of the Communist Federation of Romanian students (1956–59) he took part in reprisals against students who demonstrated in support of the Hungarian revolution. Most of Iliescu's career was spent in the Department of Ideology and Propaganda of the Communist Party culminating in his elevation to the Central Committee (1965) and appointment by Ceauşescu as First Secretary of the Union of Communist Youth and Minister for Youth Affairs (1967). In 1971 he became Secretary for Ideology of the Communist Party, only to lose his position the same year for privately questioning Ceauşescu's 'mini cultural revolution'. Moved to the provinces, notably as First Party Secretary in Iaşi, and became subsequently Head of the Council of Hydrology. Retained seat in the Central Committee until 1984 when he was demoted to position of Director of the state Technical Publishing House.

On 22 December 1989, with Ceauşescu fleeing the crowds of protestors, Iliescu took control of the state TV studios and became President of the self-appointed National Salvation Council. Elected President of Romania in May 1990 and re-elected in 1992, he ran again for President in 1996, though unsuccessfully, and is a candidate in the 2000 race.

Gabriel Liiceanu (b. 1942)
A philosopher and classical scholar, he was a pupil of Noica (see below). Researcher at the Institute of Philosophy (1965–75) and at the Institute of History of the Arts (1975–89). He was a leading dissident from 1987 onwards, with strong contacts with France. Immediately after the revolution he became director of Romania's largest independent publishing house, Humanitas, where he has remained ever since. Also professor at Bucharest University's Department of Philosophy, publishing essays and translations of Plato, Heidegger and Schelling.

Constantin Noica (1909–87)
One of Romania's most celebrated twentieth-century philosophers and essayists, he began in the 1930s as a journalist, together with Mircea Eliade and Emil Cioran. Although almost all of his intellectual contemporaries emigrated after the Communists came to power, Noica believed it his duty to remain. Exiled to the town of Campulung Muscel 1949–58 and a political prisoner 1958–64. Books and essays on Hegel, Greek philosophy, and Romania appeared when he was allowed to publish after 1965. In later years he established an informal school of philosophy in the village of Paltiniş, his star pupils being Andrei Pleşu (q.v.) and Gabriel Liiceanu (q.v.). Awarded the Herder Prize in 1988.

Andrei Pleşu (b. 1948)
Studied History and Theory of Art at Bucharest University. Lectured at Bucharest's Academy of Fine Arts from 1971. Expelled from the Communist Party and from Bucharest University in 1983, he continued with research at the Institute of the History of the Arts, at the same time taking on the role of an outspoken dissident. In 1989 he was exiled to a village in northern Moldavia after an interview with the Securitate. In 1990 he became Minister of Culture in President Iliescu's government and was, from 1997 to 1999, Romania's Minister of Foreign Affairs under President Constantinescu. Founder of the New Europe Foundation and Rector of the New Europe College, his publications include several books on art, aesthetics and philosophy. Awarded the Humbolt Medal (1998) and Goethe Medal (1999).

Index

155–7, 159, 161, 163,
164–73, 175, 177, 179, 181,
185–7, 200, 202, 208, 210,
211, 213
Budapest 95, 106, 112–14, 128,
131, 152
Buftea 164
Bukovina 128
Bulgaria 128
Bunescu, Preda 140
Burke, Edmund 27, 45, 94
Burke, Tom 142, 163
Bydgoszcz 82

Cambridge 147, 185, 187
Camus, Albert 52
Canada 194
Candole, James de 201
Cantacuzino, Sherban 128,
137, 148
Čarnogorský, Jan 124, 208
Carol, King, of Romania 201
Carson, Rachel 181
Carter, President Jimmy 129
Casanova, Giacomo 24
Ceauşescu, Elena 194
Ceauşescu, Nicolae 9, 127–9,
132–3, 137–8, 140–3, 143n,
144, 148–50, 153, 154–8,
162–3, 167, 169, 171, 176,
182, 186, 193, 194–6, 198,
200, 203, 206–7, 210–12,
214
Ceauşescu, Nicu 150
Celac, Mariana 131, 132, 133,
140–3, 148, 151, 153,
158–9, 161–4, 167–9, 171,
185–6, 202–3, 207
Celac, Sergiu 133

Cernat, Dr Manuela 167
Charles, Caroline 83
Charles IV, Emperor 67
Charles, Prince of Wales 194–5,
195, 196, 199, 200
Chernenko, Konstantin 51, 57,
88
Chernobyl 106
Chesterton, G. K. 165
Chiriac, Ion 140
Chrostowski, Waldemar 82
Cismărescu, Mihai 140
Cluj 9, 154–5, 182, 196–7, 199,
201
Constantine, Emperor 161–2
Constantinescu, Emil 9
Cook, Robin 89
Coriolanus 140
Cornea, Ariadne 182
Cornea, Doina 154–5, 174,
182, 184, 193–4, 196–9
Covaci, Aurel 170
Cox, Baroness 55–6, 62
Cracow 50, 53, 55, 131
Curry, Edwina 210
Czechoslovakia 10, 14, 17–18,
20, 21, 33, 39, 42, 44, 47,
58, 66, 70, 72, 84, 87, 90–2,
98, 101, 106, 111, 116, 119,
130, 133, 145, 162, 179,
193, 206–7
Częstochowa 52, 85

Daniels, Anthony ('Dr
Theodore Dalrymple')
203–4
Danube, River 109, 111; canal
111, 127–8, 132
Davies, Norman 49, 113